11+
Verbal Reasoning Success

Age 6–7

Age 7–8

Age 8–9

Age 9–10

Age 10–11

Assessment Papers

Alison Primrose

Sample page

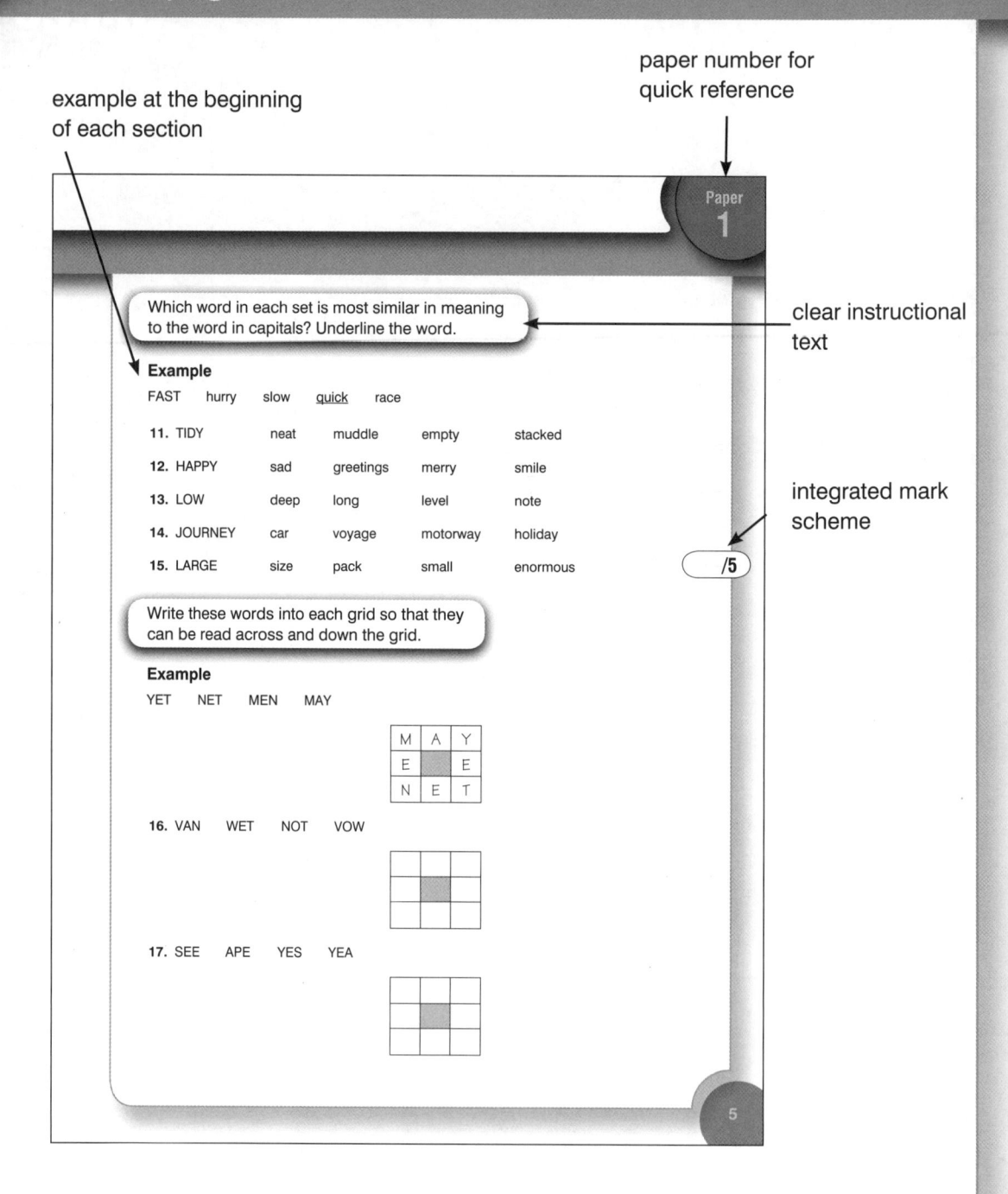

example at the beginning of each section

paper number for quick reference

Paper 1

Which word in each set is most similar in meaning to the word in capitals? Underline the word.

clear instructional text

Example

FAST   hurry   slow   <u>quick</u>   race

11. TIDY   neat   muddle   empty   stacked
12. HAPPY   sad   greetings   merry   smile
13. LOW   deep   long   level   note
14. JOURNEY   car   voyage   motorway   holiday
15. LARGE   size   pack   small   enormous

/5

integrated mark scheme

Write these words into each grid so that they can be read across and down the grid.

Example

YET   NET   MEN   MAY

M	A	Y
E		E
N	E	T

16. VAN   WET   NOT   VOW

17. SEE   APE   YES   YEA

5

Contents

PAPER 1	4
PAPER 2	8
PAPER 3	12
PAPER 4	16
PAPER 5	20
PAPER 6	23
PAPER 7	27
PAPER 8	31
PAPER 9	35
PAPER 10	39
PAPER 11	43
PAPER 12	47
PAPER 13	51
PAPER 14	55
PAPER 15	59
PAPER 16	63
PAPER 17	66
PAPER 18	70
PAPER 19	74
PAPER 20	78
PAPER 21	82
PAPER 22	86
Progress grid	90
Answer booklet	1–4

PAPER 1

Underline the two words in each set that rhyme with the word in capitals.

Example

CAT   mate   <u>mat</u>   freight   pant   <u>sat</u>

1. BANK   chalk   liken   <u>drank</u>   <u>tank</u>   ankle
2. ROUGH   <u>buff</u>   trough   <u>cuff</u>   cough   through
3. SHAVE   shiver   haven   shove   <u>knave</u>   <u>cave</u>
4. LITTER   mantra   grotto   <u>sitter</u>   ditto   <u>fritter</u>
5. VENT   lava   vein   <u>meant</u>   <u>scent</u>   servant

4/5

Which word in each set is opposite in meaning to the word in capitals? Underline the word.

Example

HOT   steaming   warm   frozen   <u>cold</u>

6. ASCEND   descent   elevator   <u>descend</u>   hill
7. BEGIN   final   close   start   <u>end</u>
8. CLEAN   <u>dirty</u>   dusty   mud   hoover
9. DIM   glow   <u>beam</u>   <u>bright</u>   bulb
10. DEEP   paddle   <u>shallow</u>   wade   depth

4/5

Paper 1

Which word in each set is most similar in meaning to the word in capitals? Underline the word.

Example
FAST   hurry   slow   <u>quick</u>   race

11. TIDY   <u>neat</u>   muddle   empty   stacked
12. HAPPY   sad   greetings   <u>merry</u>   <u>smile</u>
13. LOW   <u>deep</u>   long   level   note
14. JOURNEY   car   <u>voyage</u>   motorway   <u>holiday</u>
15. LARGE   size   pack   small   <u>enormous</u>

3/5

Write these words into each grid so that they can be read across and down the grid.

Example
YET   NET   MEN   MAY

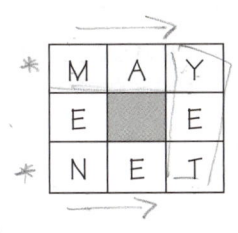

M	A	Y
E		E
N	E	T

16. VAN   WET   NOT   VOW

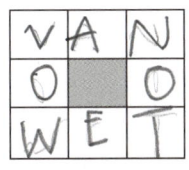

V	A	N
O		O
W	E	T

17. SEE   APE   YES   YEA

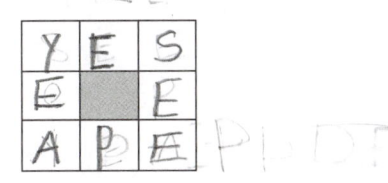

Y	E	S
E		E
A	P	E

18. KIN AMP ASK PEN

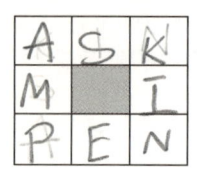

|A|S|K|
|M| |I|
|P|E|N|

19. BIT NOW TOW BUN

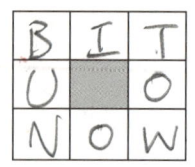

|B|I|T|
|U| |O|
|N|O|W|

20. NET TOT COT CAN

|C|O|T|
|A| |O|
|N|O|T|

5/5

> Underline the word in the brackets that completes the second pair of words in the same way as the first pair.

Example

A is to B as one is to (to, <u>two</u>, too, three).

21. Car is to four as bicycle is to (saddle, bell, <u>two</u>, helmet).

22. Pram is to baby as wheelbarrow is to (hose, shed, <u>weeds</u>, garden).

23. Glove is to hand as sock is to (boot, <u>foot</u>, shoe, stocking).

24. A is to beginning as Z is to (alphabet, zoo, <u>end</u>, last).

25. Sky is to blue as grass is to (blade, turf, <u>green</u>, lawn).

5/5

In each sentence below, rearrange the word in capitals to make a properly spelt word that completes the sentence. Write the word on the answer line.

Example

The children were late for SLOHOC.   SCHOOL

26. They had to run to CHTCA the train.   CATCH
27. The clock MECDHI every hour.   CHIMED
28. The team scored after a NPYALET was given.   PENALTY
29. A perfect holiday, lazing on the HEBCA all day.   BEACH
30. NSPUNEIG huddle together during fierce blizzards.   PENGUINS

5/5

Look carefully at these letter sequences. Work out the patterns to find the next letters in each sequence. The alphabet is here to help you.

A B C D E F G H I J K L M N O P Q R S T U V W X Y Z

Example

AB   DE   GH   JK   ?   MN

31. AC   AE   AG   AI   AK
32. TS   RQ   PO   NM   LK
33. F   FG   EFG   EFGH   DEFGH
34. GA   GB   GC   GD   GE
35. ZX   YW   XV   WU   VT

5/5

Paper 2

Look carefully at the given codes and work out the answers to the questions.

Example
If the code for SEAM is 3415, what is the code for SEA? 341

36. If the code for DEAR is 1234, what is the code for RED? 421
37. If the code for STEAM is 46321, what is the code for SAME? 4213
38. If the code for PASTE is 51234, what is the code for TAPS? 3152
39. If the code for FRESH is 46217, what is the code for HERE? 7262
40. If the code for BONES is 31524, what is the code for SOBS? 4134

5/5

36/40

PAPER 2

Which word in each set is opposite in meaning to the word in capitals? Underline the word.

Example
HOT   steaming   warm   frozen   <u>cold</u>

1. BOLD   mouse   timid   afraid   quiet
2. FAT   dumpy   lean   plump   meat
3. EARLY   night   sleep   late   moon
4. FLEXIBLE   bendy   rigid   tight   moveable
5. LEFT   starboard front   right   port

5/5

Paper 2

Which word in each set is most similar in meaning to the word in capitals? Underline the word.

Example
FAST   hurry   slow   <u>quick</u>   race

6. FANTASY   fairy   detail   (fiction)   real
7. FLOWER   (bloom)   bunch   florist   petal
8. TABLET   sick   (pill)   doctor   chemist
9. STICK   cut   lick   (paste)   paper
10. WASH   soap   cold   (clean)   water

5/5

Write these words into each grid so that they can be read across and down the grid.

Example
TOP   TIN   NAY   PAY

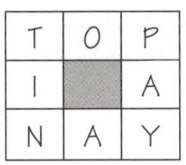

T	O	P
I		A
N	A	Y

11. DID   DAB   DON   BIN

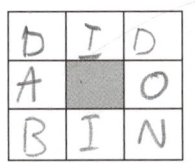

D	I	D
A		O
B	I	N

12. NOD   DIN   PAN   NIP

N	I	P
O		A
D	I	N

13. RUG   DIG   END   EAR

E	N	D
A		I
R	U	G

14. TEN   RAN   FAR   FIT

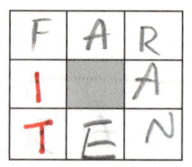

F	A	R
I		A
T	E	N

15. GOT   GIG   GAP   TAP

G	O	T
I		A
G	A	P

5/5

Underline the word in the brackets that completes the second pair of words in the same way as the first pair.

Example
A is to B as one is to (to, <u>two</u>, too, three).

16. Ice is to cold as sun is to (yellow, <u>hot,</u> rays, summer).

17. Beginning is to end as start is to (commence, finale, <u>finish,</u> extend).

18. Violin is to bow as flute is to (tune, woodwind, <u>blow</u>, music).

19. Broken is to repair as tear is to (rip, pin, <u>mend</u>, gather).

20. Apple is to orchard as grape is to (vine, fruit, <u>vineyard</u>, wine).

5/5

Paper 2

Look carefully at these letter sequences. Work out the patterns to find the next letters in each sequence. The alphabet is here to help you.

A B C D E F G H I J K L M N O P Q R S T U V W X Y Z

Example

AB DE GH JK ? __MN__

21. ST QR OP MN __KL__
22. AC EG IK MO __QS__
23. KZ LY MX __NW__ OV
24. ACB DFE GIH __JLK__ MON
25. BA DC FE HG __JI__

5/5

Look carefully at the given codes and work out the answers to the questions.

Example

If the code for SEAM is 3415, what is the code for SEA? __341__

26. If the code for STRAP is 87541, what is the code for PAST? __1487__
27. If the code for MOTEL is 36724, what is the code for TOOL? __7664__
28. If the code for CATER is 42613, what is the code for TRACE? __63241__
29. If the code for REACH is 12345, what is the code for ARCH? __3145__
30. If the code for STALE is 45321, what is the code for EAST? __1345__

5/5

In each sentence below, rearrange the word in capitals to make a properly spelt word that completes the sentence. Write the word on the answer line.

Example

The children were late for SLOHOC. __SCHOOL__

31. After six hours climbing, they reached the MIMUTS. __SUMMIT__
32. He made a drink of hot COLAHTEOC for them all. __CHOCOLATE__
33. The puppies were racing UNORD the garden. __ROUND__

34. Each week there was a CIEAPSL offer at the supermarket. __SPECIAL__
35. The school choir were practising for the CENRCOT. __CONCERT__

5/5

Underline the odd word out in each of these sets.
(Look carefully at the spelling **or** the meaning of each word.)

Example

spring   <u>flung</u>   fling   string

36. hall   tell   fell   hal<u>t</u>
37. knife   kneel   <u>gnome</u>   knit
38. bread   <u>mean</u>   spread   tread
39. white   yellow   <u>fast</u>   green
40. bird   eagle   robin   <u>swallow</u>

5/5

40/40

PAPER 3

Which word in each set is most similar in meaning to the word in capitals? Underline the word.

Example

FAST   hurry   slow   <u>quick</u>   race

1. PILE   hole   stones   <u>heap</u>   bury
2. WORTH   money   coins   expense   <u>value</u>
3. APARTMENT   house   <u>flat</u>   bungalow   palace
4. OCEAN   <u>sea</u>   stream   lake   reservoir
5. RUG   bed   <u>blanket</u>   warm   travel

5/5

Write these words into each grid so that they can be read across and down the grid.

Example

TOP   TIN   NAY   PAY

T	O	P
I		A
N	A	Y

6. POT   HIP   HEN   NOT

H	E	N
I		O
P	O	T

7. JAW   JOG   GUN   WON

J	A	W
O		O
G	U	N

8. PAW   KIP   NOW   KIN

K	I	N
I		O
P	A	W

9. GET   BIG   BAG   GOT

B	I	G
A		O
G	E	T

10. DIP   TAP   FIT   FED

F	I	T
E		A
D	I	P

5/5

Underline the word in the brackets that completes the second pair of words in the same way as the first pair.

Example

A is to B as one is to (to, <u>two</u>, too, three).

11. Sea is to waves as sky is to (blue, space, <u>clouds</u>, clear).
12. Float is to sink as wet is to (damp, soaked, <u>dry</u>, parched).
13. Jam is to tart as apple is to (tree, orchard, <u>pie</u>, core).
14. Letters is to words as numbers is to (maths, counting, money, <u>sums</u>).
15. Eyes is to see as ears is to (earring, deaf, <u>hear</u>, plugs).

5/5

In each sentence below, rearrange the word in capitals to make a properly spelt word that completes the sentence. Write the word on the answer line.

Example

The children were late for SLOHOC.   SCHOOL

16. She shared the PERCIE for the delicious chocolate cake. RECIPE
17. The children were very EDITEXC waiting for his arrival. EXCITED
18. The famous story was made into a very SCSFUCEUSL film. SUCCESSFUL
19. The little children enjoyed going to SERYUNR each day. NURSERY
20. In November, people have RENFOBI parties. BONFIRE

5/5

Look carefully at these letter sequences. Work out the patterns to find the next letters in each sequence. The alphabet is here to help you.

A B C D E F G H I J K L M N O P Q R S T U V W X Y Z

Example

AB   DE   GH   JK   ?   <u>MN</u>

21. AZ   BY   CX   DW   EV
22. GI   GK   GM   GO   GQ
23. NO   MP   LQ   KR   JS

14

24. ZYX   YXW   XWV   _WVU_
25. MA   BM   MC   DM   _ME_

5/5

Look carefully at the given codes and work out the answers to the questions.

Example

If the code for SEAM is 3415, what does the code 341 stand for?   _SEA_

If the code for PLANE is 41352:

26. What is the code for LEAP? _1234_
27. What is the code for ALP? _314_
28. What does the code 312 stand for? _ALE_

If the code for SPINE is 35749:

29. What is the code for NIPS? _4753_
30. What does the code 594 stand for? _PEN_

5/5

Underline the odd word out in each of these sets.
(Look carefully at the spelling **or** the meaning of each word.)

Example

spring   <u>flung</u>   fling   string

31. pain   ran   train   <u>pane</u>
32. <u>which</u>   white   when   will
33. chapter   book   <u>number</u>   letter
34. running   walking <u>talk</u>   singing
35. tramp   <u>ample</u>   camp   damp

5/5

Which word in each set **cannot** be made using the letters of the word in capitals? Underline the word.

Example

PLATE   tea   tape   eap   <u>pail</u>

36. BEAST   stab   beats   seat   <u>table</u>
37. CHANGE   ace   <u>chain</u>   hang   ache
38. DENTAL   deal   lane   tend   <u>tanned</u>
39. EAGLE   gale   <u>angle</u>   eel   glee
40. FRIEND   fend   rife   <u>fender</u> dine

5/5

40/40

PAPER 4

Underline the two words in each set that rhyme with the word in capitals.

Example

CAT   mate   <u>mat</u>   freight   pant   <u>sat</u>

1. MISER   wise   <u>visor</u>   misery   mirror   <u>wiser</u>
2. MONK   milk   <u>punk</u>   plonk   donkey   <u>sunk</u>
3. FASHION   nation   cash   <u>ashen</u>   cushion   <u>ration</u>
4. EAST   priest   best   weasel   create   <u>beast</u>
5. PROUD   around   flowed   <u>crowd</u>   sound   <u>loud</u>

5/5

Write these words into each grid so that they can be read across and down the grid.

Example

TOP   TIN   NAY   PAY

T	O	P
I		A
N	A	Y

6. TIN   WIN   COW   CAT

C	O	W
A		I
T	I	N

7. SOB   SEE   BYE   EYE

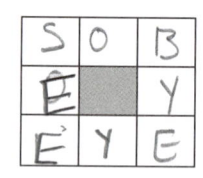

S	O	B
E		Y
E	Y	E

8. NAP FIT TOP FEN

```
F I T
E   O
N A P
```

9. DIG YAP DAY GAP

```
D I G
A   A
Y A P
```

10. SET DAY SAD TRY

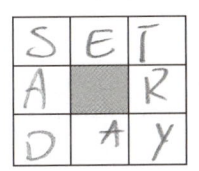

```
S E T
A   R
D A Y
```

5/5

Underline the word in the brackets that completes the second pair of words in the same way as the first pair.

Example

A is to B as one is to (to, <u>two</u>, too, three).

11. Stamp is to loud as creep is to (sneaky, tiptoe, <u>quiet</u>, dark).

12. Leap is to far as jump is to (vault, bar, mat, <u>high</u>).

13. Red is to rose as green is to (go, emerald, <u>leaf</u>, jealousy).

14. Hot is to soup as cold is to (freezer, <u>ice-cream</u>, coat, snow).

15. Bed is to lie as chair is to (relax, read, cushion, <u>sit</u>).

4/5

17

Paper 4

In each sentence below, rearrange the word in capitals to make a properly spelt word that completes the sentence. Write the word on the answer line.

Example

The children were late for SLOHOC.   SCHOOL

16. The toddlers spent hours GAYIPLN in the sandpit. PLAYING
17. The cake was CDRATODEE with icing and candles. DECORATED
18. The airport RESTUREPAD sign showed there was a delay. DEPARTURES
19. The children enjoyed the LEOSTABC race the most. OSTACLE
20. Astronauts wear special CGTNHILO when travelling in space. CLOTHING

2/5

Look carefully at these letter sequences. Work out the patterns to find the next letters in each sequence. The alphabet is here to help you.

A B C D E F G H I J K L M N O P Q R S T U V W X Y Z

Example

AB   DE   GH   JK   ?   MN

21. A10   B9   C8   D7   E6
22. VZ   UY   TX   SW   RV
23. CA   DB   EC   FD   GE
24. HIJ   JKL   LMN   NOP   PQR
25. AB   DC   EF   HG   IJ

5/5

Look carefully at the given codes and work out the answers to the questions.

Example

If the code for SEAM is 3415, what does the code 341 stand for?   SEA

If the code for SHORE is 24681:

26. What is the code for ROSE?   8621
27. What does the code 418 stand for?   HER

18

If the code for MELTS is 35421:

28. What is the code for STEM? 1253

29. What is the code for SELL? 1544

30. What does the code 452 stand for? LET

Underline the odd word out in each of these sets.
(Look carefully at the spelling **or** the meaning of each word.)

Example
spring   <u>flung</u>   fling   string

31. fly   <u>horse</u>   beetle   wasp

32. middle   central   <u>edge</u>   centre

33. string   thread   <u>sack</u>   rope

34. pool   <u>rule</u>   cool   tool

35. write   written   <u>reading</u>   wrote

Which word in each set **cannot** be made using the letters of the word in capitals? Underline the word.

Example
PLATE   tea   tape   leap   <u>pail</u>

36. GARAGE   rage   <u>argue</u>   egg   gage

37. HOARSE   horse   hears   <u>hearse</u>   shore

38. ISLAND   sail   <u>ideal</u>   sand   dials

39. JUPITER   jute   tripe   <u>jeer</u>   erupt

40. KITCHEN   itch   hike   <u>chick</u>   chin

PAPER 5

Underline the two words in each set that rhyme with the word in capitals.

Example

CAT   mate   <u>mat</u>   freight   pant   <u>sat</u>

1. COPE   choke   mop   shop   <u>scope</u>   <u>hope</u>
2. FLANNEL   tunnel   <u>channel</u>   funnel   whistle   <u>panel</u>
3. WINCH   which   inch   witch   <u>pitch</u>   <u>pinch</u>
4. MALLET   wallet   <u>pallet</u>   valet   <u>ballet</u>   ballot
5. PRAISE   rise   crease   <u>maize</u>   chase   <u>phase</u>

/5

Which word in each set is opposite in meaning to the word in capitals? Underline the word.

Example

HOT   steaming   warm   frozen   <u>cold</u>

6. BROAD   wide   <u>narrow</u>   road   valley
7. BUY   purchase   <u>sell</u>   market   cash
8. CHEAP   price   value   <u>expensive</u>   cost
9. ENTHUSIASM   energy   idle   keen   <u>apathy</u>
10. ENTRANCE   door   escape   <u>exit</u>   reception

/5

Which word in each set is most similar in meaning to the word in capitals? Underline the word.

Example

FAST   hurry   slow   <u>quick</u>   race

11. SWEEP   path   broom   bristle   <u>brush</u>
12. THIEF   <u>burglar</u>   tiptoe   robbery   swag

13. PURSE	notes	cash	coins	<u>wallet</u>	
14. ROCK	cliff	granite	<u>boulder</u>	sand	4/5
15. DISH	<u>plate</u>	cup	saucer	bowl	

In each sentence below, rearrange the word in capitals to make a properly spelt word that completes the sentence. Write the word on the answer line.

Example

The children were late for SLOHOC.   <u>SCHOOL</u>

16. The children went for NOYDKE rides along the beach. <u>DONKEY</u>
17. It was a windy day, perfect for flying TESKI. <u>KITES</u>
18. The old lady was always glad to have SORISIVT. <u>VISITORS</u>
19. They all had to go to the TISETND for a check up. <u>DENTIST</u>
20. The fairy tale ended with them all living PLAHPIY ever after. <u>HAPPILY</u>

5/5

Look carefully at these letter sequences. Work out the patterns to find the next letters in each sequence. The alphabet is here to help you.

A B C D E F G H I J K L M N O P Q R S T U V W X Y Z

Example

AB   DE   GH   JK   ?   <u>MN</u>

21. AA   BC   DD   EF   GG   <u>HI</u>
22. MO   NP   OQ   PR   <u>QS</u>
23. GZ   FY   EX   <u>DW</u>   CV
24. WVU   TSR   QPO   NML   <u>KJI</u>
25. LK   IJ   HG   EF   <u>DC</u>   AB

5/5

Paper 5

Look carefully at the given codes and work out the answers to the questions.

Example

If the code for SEAM is 3415, what does the code 341 stand for?   SEA

If the code for READS is 32415:

26. What is the code for DARE?   1432
27. What is the code for SEA?   523   ~~524~~
28. What does the code 321 stand for?   RED

If the code for MITRE is 76541:

29. What is the code for TIME?   5671
30. What is the code for MERIT?   71465

4/5

Underline the odd word out in each of these sets.
(Look carefully at the spelling **or** the meaning of each word.)

Example

spring   <u>flung</u>   fling   string

31. plastic   wood   <u>building</u>   stone
32. ruby   emerald   <u>lead</u>   diamond
33. tune   <u>orchestra</u>   melody   music
34. half   third   <u>division</u>   quarter
35. rewind   return   reprint   <u>red</u>

4/5

Which word in each set **cannot** be made using the letters of the word in capitals? Underline the word.

Example

PLATE   tea   tape   leap   <u>pail</u>

36. LANTERN   antler   <u>relate</u>   later   tale
37. MAGICAL   claim   clam   mail   <u>cigar</u>
38. NETTLE   let   <u>enter</u>   ten   lent
39. OPERA   reap   pore   <u>open</u>   pear
40. POETRY   <u>reply</u>   pry   try   opt

5/5

37/40

PAPER 6

Underline the two words in each set that rhyme with the word in capitals.

Example

CAT   mate   <u>mat</u>   freight   pant   <u>sat</u>

1. MOTION   <u>lotion</u>   faction   <u>notion</u>   nation   mention
2. LETTER   mitre   <u>better</u>   flutter   beater   <u>setter</u>
3. WAGON   argon   <u>lagoon</u>   <u>flagon</u>   dragon   jargon
4. WEDGE   ridge   midget   <u>hedge</u>   <u>pledge</u>   fridge
5. MILE   mill   <u>style</u>   veil   <u>dial</u>   sigh

5 /5

Which word in each set is opposite in meaning to the word in capitals? Underline the word.

Example

HOT   steaming   warm   frozen   <u>cold</u>

6. RAW   frozen   <u>cooked</u>   fresh   boil
7. RELAXED   sleepy   rested   angry   <u>tense</u>
8. SINK   <u>float</u>   drown   heavy   drift
9. SMOOTH   level   hill   bumpy   flat
10. PROFESSIONAL   proper   <u>amateur</u>   beginner   student

5 /5

Which word in each set is most similar in meaning to the word in capitals? Underline the word.

Example

FAST   hurry   slow   <u>quick</u>   race

11. MIX   bowl   <u>stir</u>   water   mixture
12. CAKE   slice   tea   <u>gateau</u>   biscuit
13. PAINTING   red   frame   <u>picture</u>   brush
14. RAMBLE   run   <u>walk</u>   marathon   skip
15. ANCIENT   ruin   grey   <u>old</u>   castle

5/5

Write these words into each grid so that they can be read across and down the grid.

Example

TOP   TIN   NAY   PAY

T	O	P
I		A
N	A	Y

16. PIE   TIE   TIP   EWE

T	I	E
I		W
P	I	E

17. SHE   WAS   OWE   WOO

W	A	S
O		H
O	W	E

18. CUB   CAP   POT   BIT

C	U	B
A		I
P	O	T

19. NIT   PUT   GAP   GUN

G	A	P
U		U
N	I	T

20. TON   HAT   MAN   HAM

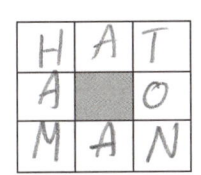

H	A	T
A		O
M	A	N

5/5

> Underline the word in the brackets that completes the second pair of words in the same way as the first pair.

Example

A is to B as one is to (to, <u>two</u>, too, three).

21. Door is to house as gate is to (fence, road, <u>garden</u>, bolt).

22. Front is to back as top is to (high, wide, low, <u>bottom</u>).

23. North is to south as east is to (sunrise, China, <u>west</u>, directions).

24. Heron is to fish as squirrel is to (tree, branch, drey, <u>nuts</u>).

25. Two is to half as four is to (share, thirds, <u>quarter</u>, piece).

5/5

25

Paper 6

Look carefully at the given codes and work out the answers to the questions.

Example

If the code for SEAM is 3415, what does the code 341 stand for? <u>SEA</u>

If the code for SPEED is 42331:

26. What is the code for DEEP? <u>1332</u>

27. What does the code 433 stand for? <u>SEE</u>

If the code for STOAT is 15245:

28. What is the code for SOOT? <u>1225</u>

29. What is the code for TOAST? <u>52415</u>

30. What does the code 145 stand for? <u>SAT</u>

5/5

Underline the odd word out in each of these sets.
(Look carefully at the spelling **or** the meaning of each word.)

Example

spring   <u>flung</u>   fling   string

31. cartoon   moon   bassoon   <u>moan</u>

32. rubies   <u>valleys</u>   babies   ladies

33. coat   jacket   blazer   <u>bread</u>

34. oak   <u>strawberry</u>   ash   sycamore

35. morning   evening   <u>autumn</u>   afternoon

5/5

Which word in each set **cannot** be made using the letters of the word in capitals? Underline the word.

Example

PLATE   tea   tape   leap   pail

36. QUESTION   quins   quoin   stone   strong
37. RAINBOW   brown   warns   brain   barn
38. STRANGER ranger angry   great   garnets
39. TRIANGLE grain   range   eager   angle
40. UMBRELLA bull   plumber bale   marble

5/5

40/40

PAPER 7

Underline (circle) the two words in each set that rhyme with the word in capitals.

Example

CAT   mate   mat   freight   pant   sat

1. POCKET   locket   locker   socket   pickle   packet
2. SPADE   maid   pad   wader   played   said
3. MIGHTY   nightie light   weighty nightly flighty
4. RATE   bait   coat   fete   cart   tare
5. WINED   fine   bind   dined   whine   dinner

5/5

Paper 7

Which word in each set is opposite in meaning to the word in capitals? Underline the word.

Example
HOT   steaming   warm   frozen   <u>cold</u>

6. SILENT   quiet   (noisy)   cheer   crash
7. SIMPLE   average   busy   easy   (complex)
8. FOCUSED   vision   stare   (blurred)   clear
9. GIANT   big   (dwarf)   size   star
10. GIVE   promise   offer   (take)   donate

5/5

Which word in each set is most similar in meaning to the word in capitals? Underline the word.

Example
FAST   hurry   slow   <u>quick</u>   race

11. STONE   <u>pebble</u>   stream   tree   pipe
12. ALONE   crowd   enemy   friends   (solitary)
13. FIRE   wood   (flame)   heat   coal
14. SEAT   table   shelter   (chair)   curtains
15. CARPET   <u>floor</u>   hoover   slippers   (rug)

4/5

Write these words into each grid so that they can be read across and down the grid.

Example
TOP   TIN   NAY   PAY

T	O	P
I		A
N	A	Y

28

16. WIT   JOG   GOT   JEW

J	O	G
E		O
W	I	T

17. GUN   LOG   PIN   LIP

L	I	P
O		I
G	U	N

18. WON   TEN   MAT   MOW

M	A	T
O		E
W	O	N

19. FIN   OFF   TEN   OFT

O	F	F
F		I
T	E	N

20. BAG   WIT   BOW   GOT

B	A	G
O		O
W	I	T

5/5

Underline the word in the brackets that completes the second pair of words in the same way as the first pair.

Example

A is to B as one is to (to, <u>two</u>, too, three).

21. Steep is to hill as level is to (exam, grade, <u>plain</u>, field).

22. Car is to drive as aeroplane is to (travel, <u>fly</u>, distant, airport).

23. Sugary is to sweet as salty is to (sea, crisps, pepper, savoury).

24. Above is to below as on is to (table, top, under, cloth).

25. Milk is to drop as bread is to (loaf, sandwich, yeast, crumb).

4/5

In each sentence below, rearrange the word in capitals to make a properly spelt word that completes the sentence. Write the word on the answer line.

Example

The children were late for SLOHOC.   SCHOOL

26. The amazing first prize was a ARASFI holiday in Africa. SAFRI *(A)* — SAFARI

27. The family POGTHRHOSAP were carefully stuck into the album. PHOTOGIRAPS — Photographs

28. It was easy getting tickets through the NETIERNT. INRENT — INTERNET

29. He liked to read the daily PSPEEWNAR each evening. NEWSPAPER

30. What is your favourite ABATEKFRS cereal? BREAKFAST

3/5

Look carefully at these letter sequences. Work out the patterns to find the next letters in each sequence. The alphabet is here to help you.

A B C D E F G H I J K L M N O P Q R S T U V W X Y Z

Example

AB   DE   GH   JK   ?   MN

31. BD   FH   JL   NP   R T
32. ZA   YC   XE   WG   V I
33. ABA   CDC   EFE   GHG   I J I
34. MZ   LY   KX   JW   I V
35. AZ   BZ   CY   D Y   EX   FX

5/5

Paper 8

Which word in each set **cannot** be made using the letters of the word in capitals? Underline the word.

Example
PLATE   tea   tape   leap   <u>pail</u>

36. VOLUME   move   mule   (oval)   love
37. WEATHER   wrath   heart   thaw   <u>waiter</u>
38. APPLES   <u>please</u>   lapse   leap   slap
39. BROKEN   born   bone   <u>brink</u>   robe
40. CAVERN   raven   cane   near   <u>crate</u>

5/5

36/40

PAPER 8

Which word in each set is most similar in meaning to the word in capitals? Underline the word.

Example
FAST   hurry   slow   <u>quick</u>   race

1. MISLAID   found   dropped   (lost)   forgotten
2. DISCOVER   <u>find</u>   hunt   search   seek
3. START   end   progress   last   <u>begin</u>
4. WINNER   competition   <u>victor</u>   race   prize
5. COARSE   flat   <u>rough</u>   smooth   soft

5/5

Paper 8

Write these words into each grid so that they can be read across and down the grid.

Example

TOP   TIN   NAY   PAY

T	O	P
I		A
N	A	Y

6. SKI   PEN   INN   SIP

S	K	I
I		N
P	E	N

7. PIT   AMP   ALL   LET

A	M	P
L		I
L	E	T

8. DRY   RAY   FOR   FED

F	O	R
E		A
D	R	Y

9. EAR   ERR   OWE   ORE

O	W	E
R		A
E	R	R

10. COT   CAP   PEA   TEA

C	O	T
A		E
P	E	A

/5

Paper 8

Underline the word in the brackets that completes the second pair of words in the same way as the first pair.

Example
A is to B as one is to (to, <u>two</u>, too, three).

11. Bees is to hive as birds is to (egg, <u>nest</u>, feather, flock).
12. Pack is to wolves as flock is to (shepherd, gather, cats, <u>sheep</u>).
13. Minute is to hour as centimetre is to (ruler, yard, <u>metre</u>, size).
14. Raw is to cooked as fresh is to (new, <u>stale</u>, wet, cold).
15. Visible is to invisible as seen is to (spotted, glasses, found, <u>unseen</u>).

5/5

In each sentence below, rearrange the word in capitals to make a properly spelt word that completes the sentence. Write the word on the answer line.

Example
The children were late for SLOHOC.   SCHOOL

16. He hit his head when he fell off the OBONTGAG in the snow. TOBOGGAN ?
17. They had learned about ETNSAMG in their science lesson. MAGNETS
18. Red, yellow and blue are the three RYMRAPI colours. PRIMARY
19. She was very MAOFUS after winning the round-the-world yacht race. FAMOUS
20. The AETSHLTE were warming up before the race. ATHLETES

4/5

Look carefully at these letter sequences. Work out the patterns to find the next letters in each sequence. The alphabet is here to help you.

A B C D E F G H I J K L M N O P Q R S T U V W X Y Z

Example
AB   DE   GH   JK   ?   <u>MN</u>

21. AC   BD   CE   DF   <u>EG</u>
22. BE   HK   NQ   <u>TX TW</u>   ZC

33

23. LE   MF   NG   OH   __PI__
24. QQ   PR   OS   NT   __MU__
25. AZ   BA   CZ   DA   __EZ__

4/5

Look carefully at the given codes and work out the answers to the questions.

Example

If the code for SEAM is 3415, what does the code 341 stand for?   __SEA__

If the code for PRIDE is 24513:   _24513_

26. What is the code for DRIP? __1452__

27. What does the code 431 stand for? __RED__

If the code for PHONE is 46371:   _46371_

28. What is the code for ONE? __371__

29. What is the code for HOPE? __6341__

30. What does the code 617 stand for? __HEN__

5/5

Underline the odd word out in each of these sets.
(Look carefully at the spelling **or** the meaning of each word.)

Example

spring   <u>flung</u>   fling   string

31. centipede   centigrade   <u>scent</u>   centimetre

32. disagreeable   distaste   disaster   <u>dangerous</u>

33. make   <u>flick</u>   fake   sake

34. stream   river   <u>mountain</u>   canal

35. <u>short</u>   huge   large   big

5/5

Which word in each set **cannot** be made using the letters of the word in capitals? Underline the word.

Example
PLATE   tea   tape   leap   <u>pail</u>

36. DIAMOND   main   maid   domain   <u>mined</u>
37. ENGINES   <u>green</u>   gin   nine   sing
38. FLOATED   loaf   <u>fleet</u>   deaf   fated
39. GRAPES   gape   grasp   pages   <u>pangs</u>
40. HOPEFUL   pole   hole   <u>hull</u>   flop

5/5

38/40

PAPER 9

Underline the two words in each set that rhyme with the word in capitals.

Example
CAT   mate   <u>mat</u>   freight   pant   <u>sat</u>

1. PAINT   <u>saint</u>   want   <u>feint</u>   tint   pate
2. COIN   joist   <u>join</u>   reign   <u>groin</u>   doing
3. BUS   <u>fuss</u>   dust   <u>pus</u>   most   cusp
4. PRINTER   winter   lintel   twitter   <u>splinter</u>   finger
5. HOUR   four   <u>power</u>   cover   <u>shower</u>   lower

5/5

Paper 9

> Which word in each set is opposite in meaning to the word in capitals? Underline the word.

Example

HOT   steaming   warm   frozen   <u>cold</u>

6. WIDE   shallow   broad   <u>narrow</u>   open
7. HAPPY   smile   laugh   frown   <u>sad</u>
8. MORNING   dark   light   early   <u>evening</u>
9. NOISY   loud   <u>quiet</u>   bang   sound
10. HIGH   level   above   <u>low</u>   gruff

5/5

> Underline the word in the brackets that completes the second pair of words in the same way as the first pair.

Example

A is to B as one is to (to, <u>two</u>, too, three).

11. Twins is to duo as triplets is to (three, two, identical, <u>trio</u>).
12. Violin is to high as double bass is to (large, <u>low</u>, strings, loud).
13. Football is to pitch as tennis is to (racket, game, <u>court</u>, ball).
14. Speck is to dust as grain is to (pebbles, <u>sand</u>, bucket, flour).
15. Boots is to winter as sandals is to (hot, beach, toes, <u>summer</u>).

5/5

> In each sentence below, rearrange the word in capitals to make a properly spelt word that completes the sentence. Write the word on the answer line.

Example

The children were late for SLOHOC.   <u>SCHOOL</u>

16. The SRULIRQE remembered where the nuts were hidden. <u>SQUIRREL</u>
17. There were signs that the COVAOLN was about to erupt. <u>VOLCANO</u>

18. Swimming with the SPHILDON was an amazing experience. DOLPHINS
19. He was so excited to get a IKETCT for the cup final. TICKET
20. Each year, the family stayed on the DAILNS. ISLAND

5/5

Look carefully at these letter sequences. Work out the patterns to find the next letters in each sequence. The alphabet is here to help you.

A B C D E F G H I J K L M N O P Q R S T U V W X Y Z

Example

AB DE GH JK ? MN

21. AR BS CT DU **EV**
22. AZ YX WV **UT** SR
23. FM GN HO IP **JQ**
24. ZX WU TR **QO** NL
25. AD GJ MP **SV** YB

5/5

Look carefully at the given codes and work out the answers to the questions.

Example

If the code for SEAM is 3415, what does the code 341 stand for? SEA

If the code for CRAMP is 46521:

26. What is the code for PRAM? **1652**
27. What does the code 451 stand for? **CAP**

If the code for PLACE is 52913:

28. What is the code for CLAP? **1295**
29. What is the code for CELL? **1322**
30. What does the code 2395 stand for? **LEAP**

6/5

Paper 9

Underline the odd word out in each of these sets.
(Look carefully at the spelling **or** the meaning of each word.)

Example
spring   <u>flung</u>   fling   string

31. flash   crash   <u>brush</u>   trash
32. splendid   <u>stroke</u>   split   splash
33. frog   <u>eagle</u>   toad   newt
34. bread   biscuit   <u>plate</u>   cake
35. run   jump   hop   <u>metal</u>

5/5

Which word in each set **cannot** be made using the letters of the word in capitals? Underline the word.

Example
PLATE   tea   tape   leap   <u>pail</u>

36. INSTANT   taint   <u>antics</u>   stain   saint
37. JOINER   ore   rejoin   <u>joint</u>   rein
38. KESTREL   elk   steer   <u>kernel</u>   leek
39. LEOPARD   pored   <u>draped</u>   pared   polar
40. MOUNTAIN   main   <u>stain</u>   omit   tan

5/5

40/40

PAPER 10

Underline the two words in each set that rhyme with the word in capitals.

Example

CAT   mate   <u>mat</u>   freight   pant   <u>sat</u>

1. LITTLE   <u>brittle</u>   title   <u>whittle</u>   witter   lentil
2. TREE   <u>she</u>   sheep   deal   keel   <u>key</u>
3. ROOF   whiff   <u>hoof</u>   <u>proof</u>   soft   wolf
4. HONEY   <u>money</u>   bonny   bony   <u>bunny</u>   they
5. DONATION   <u>creation</u>   mention   selection   deletion   <u>foundation</u>

5/5

Which word in each set is opposite in meaning to the word in capitals? Underline the word.

Example

HOT   steaming   warm   frozen   <u>cold</u>

6. LIGHT   bright   black   <u>dark</u>   sheep
7. INCREASE   more   <u>decrease</u>   least   ascend
8. OPEN   exit   doorway   enter   <u>close</u>
9. PATTERNED   <u>plain</u>   design   relief   colour
10. COVER   protect   hide   <u>expose</u>   find

5/5

Write these words into each grid so that they can be read across and down the grid.

Example

TOP   TIN   NAY   PAY

T	O	P
I		A
N	A	Y

11. SOW   SAD   DIG   WIG

|S|O|W|
|A| |I|
|D|I|G|

12. FED   FIN   DOT   NET

|F|E|D|
|I| |O|
|N|E|T|

13. MAD   DIN   WIN   MEW

|M|A|D|
|E| |I|
|W|I|N|

14. POT   TAP   PIT   TIP

|P|O|T|
|I| |A|
|T|I|P|

15. DEW   COD   CAT   TOW

|C|O|D|
|A| |E|
|T|O|W|

/5

Underline the word in the brackets that completes the second pair of words in the same way as the first pair.

Example

A is to B as one is to (to, <u>two</u>, too, three).

16. Raspberry is to red as lemon is to (fresh, jelly, flavour, <u>yellow</u>).

17. Cup is to saucer as knife is to (cut, mug, <u>fork</u>, cutlery).

18. Scale is to salmon as fur is to (coat, warm, fox, soft).

19. Solar is to sun as lunar is to (mouth, calendar, moon, cycle).

20. Cattle is to grass as chickens is to (eggs, milk, corn, drumsticks).

/5

In each sentence below, rearrange the word in capitals to make a properly spelt word that completes the sentence. Write the word on the answer line.

Example

The children were late for SLOHOC.   SCHOOL

21. They met the local HOUTAR when visiting the library. AUTHOR

22. He was training hard ready for the CSOMPLYI. OLYMPICS

23. The airport STYURECI officers checked every bag thoroughly. SECURITY

24. ERJTUPI is one of the planets circling round the sun. JUPITER

25. There was a great offer in the GANAZIME last week. MAGAZINE

5/5

Look carefully at these letter sequences. Work out the patterns to find the next letters in each sequence. Write them on the answer line. The alphabet is here to help you.

A B C D E F G H I J K L M N O P Q R S T U V W X Y Z

Example

AB   DE   GH   JK   ?   MN

26. TU   TS   TV   TR   TW

27. CA   DB   EC   FD   GE

28. BC   AB   ZA   YZ   XY

29. XW   TS   PO   LK   HG

30. MA   NC   OE   PG   QI

5/5

Paper 10

> Look carefully at the given codes and work out the answers to the questions.

Example

If the code for SEAM is 3415, what does the code 341 stand for? <u>SEA</u>

If the code for CHORE is 54321:

31. What is the code for OCHRE? __35421__

32. What does the code 412 stand for? __HER__

If the code for FIELDS is 135426:

33. What does the code 6544 stand for? __SELL__

34. What is the code for FILES? __13456__

35. What does the code 1452 stand for? __FLED__

5/5

> Which word in each set **cannot** be made using the letters of the word in capitals on the left? Underline the word.

Example

PLATE   tea   tape   leap   <u>pail</u>

36. NOTELET   nettle   <u>outlet</u>   tent   lent

37. ORANGES   <u>ranger</u>   organs   sore   sang

38. PLASTIC   claps   <u>castle</u>   list   cast

39. REASON   nose   near   sonar   <u>answer</u>

40. SPLENDID   lend   <u>denied</u>   send   piled

5/5

40/40

PAPER 11

Underline the two words in each set that rhyme with the word in capitals.

Example

CAT   mate   <u>mat</u>   freight   pant   <u>sat</u>

1. HEDGE   <u>wedge</u>   gadget   plague   fudge   <u>sedge</u>
2. TONGUE   queue   <u>sung</u>   triangle   <u>rung</u>   through
3. MILK   <u>silk</u>   wilt   pink   bulk   <u>ilk</u>
4. COACH   <u>broach</u>   couch   <u>poach</u>   paunch   reach
5. TABLE   foible   <u>cable</u>   tablet   <u>label</u>   treble

5/5

Which word in each set is opposite in meaning to the word in capitals? Underline the word.

Example

HOT   steaming   warm   frozen   <u>cold</u>

6. STOP   red   end   <u>start</u>   sign
7. STRONG   tea   firm   bend   <u>weak</u>
8. UP   along   over   <u>down</u>   around
9. YOUNG   juvenile   baby   <u>old</u>   senior
10. ORDER   <u>chaos</u>   series   pattern   law

5/5

Which word in each set is most similar in meaning to the word in capitals? Underline the word.

Example

FAST   hurry   slow   <u>quick</u>   race

11. OAR   canoe   cover   <u>paddle</u>   speed
12. RUBBER   pencil   <u>eraser</u>   mistake   drawing
13. TIN   pot   drink   beans   <u>can</u>
14. DOZE   tires   rest   <u>snooze</u>   breath
15. LAUGH   frown   <u>chuckle</u>   grimace   tickle

5/5

43

Paper 11

Write these words into each grid so that they can be read across and down the grid.

Example

TOP TIN NAY PAY

T	O	P
I		A
N	A	Y

16. MEN TON HIM HOT

H	I	M
O		E
T	O	N

17. HUB HIM BOW MOW

H	U	B
I		O
M	O	W

18. DON DID DOT NUT

D	O	N
I		U
D	O	T

19. WIT LOP LAW PAT

L	A	W
O		I
P	A	T

20. MAY MOB YES BUS

M	A	Y
O		E
B	U	S

5/5

44

Underline the word in the brackets that completes the second pair of words in the same way as the first pair.

Example
A is to B as one is to (to, <u>two</u>, too, three).

21. Hot is to boiling as cold is to (ice, fridge, <u>freezing</u>, winter).

22. Kangaroo is to jumping as horse is to (saddle, neighing, <u>galloping</u>, hoof).

23. Thread is to string as string is to (anchor, chain, cotton, <u>rope</u>).

24. School is to teacher as college is to (lecture, student, <u>lecturer</u>, notes).

25. Weathervane is to wind direction as thermometer is to (rainfall, wind-speed, wind, <u>temperature</u>).

4 /5

Look carefully at these letter sequences. Work out the patterns to find the next letters in each sequence. The alphabet is here to help you.

A B C D E F G H I J K L M N O P Q R S T U V W X Y Z

Example
AB   DE   GH   JK   ?   <u>MN</u>

26. AM   BN   CO   DP   EQ
27. DE   DF   GH   GI   JK   JL
28. VT   US   TR   SQ   RP
29. AD   EH   IL   MP   QT
30. RA   BR   RC   DR   RE

5 /5

Paper 11

Underline the odd word out in each of these sets.
(Look carefully at the spelling **or** the meaning of each word.)

Example

spring   <u>flung</u>   fling   string

31. head   arm   <u>shoe</u>   shoulder
32. boat   <u>plane</u>   yacht   canoe
33. prime   press   praise   <u>parrot</u>
34. fellow   bellow   mellow   <u>below</u>
35. try   fry   <u>die</u>   cry

/5

Which word in each set **cannot** be made using the letters of the word in capitals? Underline the word.

Example

PLATE   tea   tape   leap   <u>pail</u>

36. TRICEPS   price   <u>pricier</u>   ices   strip
37. WINTER   twin   twine   <u>toner</u>   writ
38. ANTELOPE   elope   <u>latent</u>   leap   lane
39. BLADES   bead   <u>leased</u>   bales   sable
40. CLIMBER   lime   mile   <u>bear</u>   limber

/5

/40

Answer booklet: Verbal Reasoning age 8–9

Paper 1
1. drank, tank
2. buff, cuff
3. knave, cave
4. fritter, sitter
5. meant, scent
6. descend
7. end
8. dirty
9. bright
10. shallow
11. neat
12. merry
13. deep
14. voyage
15. enormous

Answers may vary:
16.
V	A	N
O		O
W	E	T

17.
Y	E	A
E		P
S	E	E

18.
A	M	P
S		E
K	I	N

19.
B	I	T
U		O
N	O	W

20.
C	O	T
A		O
N	E	T

21. two
22. weeds
23. foot
24. end
25. green
26. CATCH
27. CHIMED
28. PENALTY
29. BEACH
30. PENGUINS
31. AI
32. LK
33. DEFGH
34. GE
35. VT
36. 421
37. 4213
38. 3152
39. 7262
40. 4134

Paper 2
1. timid
2. lean
3. late
4. rigid
5. right
6. fiction
7. bloom
8. pill
9. paste
10. clean

Answers may vary:
11.
D	I	D
A		O
B	I	N

12.
N	O	D
I		I
P	A	N

13.
E	A	R
N		U
D	I	G

14.
F	A	R
I		A
T	E	N

15.
G	I	G
O		A
T	A	P

16. hot
17. finish
18. blow
19. mend
20. vineyard
21. KL
22. QS
23. NW
24. JLK
25. JI
26. 1487
27. 7664

28. 63241
29. 3145
30. 1345
31. SUMMIT
32. CHOCOLATE
33. ROUND
34. SPECIAL
35. CONCERT
36. halt
37. gnome
38. mean
39. fast
40. bird

Paper 3
1. heap
2. value
3. flat
4. sea
5. blanket

Answers may vary:
6.
H	I	P
E		O
N	O	T

7.
J	A	W
O		O
G	U	N

8.
K	I	N
I		O
P	A	W

9.
B	I	G
A		E
G	O	T

10.
F	I	T
E		A
D	I	P

11. clouds
12. dry
13. pie
14. sums
15. hear
16. RECIPE
17. EXCITED
18. SUCCESSFUL
19. NURSERY
20. BONFIRE
21. EV
22. GQ
23. JS
24. WVU
25. ME
26. 1234
27. 314
28. ALE
29. 4753
30. PEN
31. ran
32. will
33. number
34. talk
35. ample
36. table
37. chain
38. tanned
39. angle
40. fender

Paper 4
1. visor, wiser
2. punk, sunk
3. ashen, ration
4. priest, beast
5. crowd, loud

Answers may vary:
6.
C	A	T
O		I
W	I	N

7.
S	O	B
E		Y
E	Y	E

8.
F	I	T
E		O
N	A	P

9.
D	I	G
A		A
Y	A	P

10.
S	E	T
A		R
D	A	Y

11. quiet
12. high
13. leaf
14. ice-cream
15. sit
16. PLAYING
17. DECORATED
18. DEPARTURES
19. OBSTACLE
20. CLOTHING
21. E6
22. RV
23. GE
24. PQR
25. IJ
26. 8621
27. HER
28. 1253
29. 1544
30. LET
31. horse
32. edge
33. sack
34. rule
35. reading
36. argue
37. hearse
38. ideal
39. jeer
40. chick

Paper 5
1. scope, hope
2. channel, panel
3. inch, pinch
4. pallet, ballot
5. maize, phase
6. narrow
7. sell
8. expensive
9. apathy
10. exit
11. brush
12. burglar
13. wallet
14. boulder
15. bowl
16. DONKEY
17. KITES
18. VISITORS
19. DENTIST
20. HAPPILY
21. HI
22. QS
23. DW
24. KJI
25. DC
26. 1432
27. 524
28. RED
29. 5671
30. 71465
31. building
32. lead
33. orchestra
34. division
35. red
36. relate
37. cigar
38. enter
39. open
40. reply

Paper 6
1. lotion, notion
2. better, setter
3. flagon, dragon
4. hedge, pledge
5. style, dial
6. cooked
7. tense
8. float
9. bumpy
10. amateur
11. stir
12. gateau
13. picture
14. walk
15. old

Answers may vary:
16.
T	I	E
I		W
P	I	E

17.
W	O	O
A		W
S	H	E

18.
C	A	P
U		O
B	I	T

19.
G	A	P
U		U
N	I	T

8.
F	E	D
O		R
R	A	Y

9.
O	W	E
R		R
E	A	R

13.
M	E	W
A		I
D	I	N

14.
P	O	T
I		A
T	I	P

20.
H	A	M
A		A
T	O	N

10.
C	A	P
O		E
T	E	A

15.
C	O	D
A		E
T	O	W

21. garden **22.** bottom
23. west **24.** nuts
25. quarter **26.** 1332
27. SEE **28.** 1225
29. 52415 **30.** SAT
31. moan **32.** valleys
33. bread **34.** strawberry
35. autumn **36.** strong
37. warns **38.** angry
39. eager **40.** plumber

11. nest **12.** sheep
13. metre **14.** stale
15. unseen **16.** TOBOGGAN
17. MAGNETS **18.** PRIMARY
19. FAMOUS **20.** ATHLETES
21. EG **22.** TW
23. PI **24.** MU
25. EZ **26.** 1452
27. RED **28.** 371
29. 6341 **30.** HEN
31. scent **32.** dangerous
33. flick **34.** mountain
35. short **36.** mined
37. green **38.** fleet
39. pangs **40.** hull

16. yellow **17.** fork
18. fox **19.** moon
20. corn **21.** AUTHOR
22. OLYMPICS **23.** SECURITY
24. JUPITER **25.** MAGAZINE
26. TW **27.** GE
28. XY **29.** HG
30. QI **31.** 35421
32. HER **33.** SELL
34. 13456 **35.** FLED
36. outlet **37.** ranger
38. castle **39.** answer
40. denied

Paper 7
1. locket, socket
2. maid, played
3. nightie, flighty
4. bait, fete
5. bind, dined
6. noisy **7.** complex
8. blurred **9.** dwarf
10. take **11.** pebble
12. solitary **13.** flame
14. chair **15.** rug
Answers may vary:

16.
J	O	G
E		O
W	I	T

17.
L	I	P
O		I
G	U	N

18.
M	O	W
A		O
T	E	N

19.
O	F	T
F		E
F	I	N

20.
B	O	W
A		I
G	O	T

21. plain **22.** fly
23. savoury **24.** under
25. crumb **26.** SAFARI
27. PHOTOGRAPHS
28. INTERNET
29. NEWSPAPER
30. BREAKFAST
31. RT **32.** VI
33. IJI **34.** IV
35. DY **36.** oval
37. waiter **38.** please
39. brink **40.** crate

Paper 8
1. lost **2.** find
3. begin **4.** victor
5. rough
Answers may vary:

6.
S	I	P
K		E
I	N	N

7.
A	M	P
L		I
L	E	T

Paper 9
1. saint, feint
2. join, groin
3. fuss, pus
4. winter, splinter
5. power, shower
6. narrow **7.** sad
8. evening **9.** quiet
10. low **11.** trio
12. low **13.** court
14. sand **15.** summer
16. SQUIRREL **17.** VOLCANO
18. DOLPHINS **19.** TICKET
20. ISLAND **21.** EV
22. UT **23.** JQ
24. QO **25.** SV
26. 1652 **27.** CAP
28. 1295 **29.** 1322
30. LEAP **31.** brush
32. stroke **33.** eagle
34. plate **35.** metal
36. antics **37.** joint
38. kernel **39.** draped
40. slain

Paper 10
1. brittle, whittle
2. she, key
3. hoof, proof
4. money, bunny
5. creation, foundation
6. dark **7.** decrease
8. close **9.** plain
10. expose
Answers may vary:

11.
S	A	D
O		I
W	I	G

12.
F	E	D
I		O
N	E	T

Paper 11
1. wedge, sedge
2. sung, rung
3. silk, ilk
4. broach, poach
5. cable, label
6. start **7.** weak
8. down **9.** old
10. chaos **11.** paddle
12. eraser **13.** can
14. snooze **15.** chuckle
Answers may vary:

16.
H	I	M
O		E
T	O	N

17.
H	I	M
U		O
B	O	W

18.
D	O	N
I		U
D	O	T

19.
L	A	W
O		I
P	A	T

20.
M	A	Y
O		E
B	U	S

21. freezing **22.** galloping
23. rope **24.** lecturer
25. temperature **26.** EQ
27. JK **28.** RP
29. QT **30.** RE
31. shoe **32.** plane
33. parrot **34.** below
35. die **36.** pricier
37. toner **38.** latent
39. leased **40.** bear

Paper 12
1. cater, later **2.** mettle, petal
3. flint, dint **4.** wait, mate
5. cost, lost **6.** smooth
7. whisper **8.** winter
9. false **10.** tame
11. sob **12.** ask

13. branch 14. poison
15. gift
Answers may vary:

16.
B	I	T
I	U	
N	I	B

17.
T	I	P
	W	I
O	W	E

18.
B	U	S
U		
N	I	B

19.
M	A	N
	U	U
D	O	T

20.
C	A	R
U		A
B	A	T

21. SKIPPING 22. FOUNTAIN
23. VICTORY 24. VEGETABLES
25. COMPUTER
26. 3154 27. 1541
28. STAFF 29. 7422
30. SLAT 31. courage
32. valley 33. ounce
34. uncle 35. menu
36. nose 37. land
38. miles 39. local
40. hall

Paper 13
1. risen, wizen
2. treason, season
3. castor, plaster
4. drop, shop
5. white, height
6. modern 7. white
8. wild 9. shiny
10. west 11. broth
12. old 13. think
14. seek 15. fright
Answers may vary:

16.
N	I	L
O		O
W	I	T

17.
O	W	N
R		O
E	A	T

18.
H	I	T
E		O
M	O	W

19.
R	I	G
O		E
W	E	T

20.
N	U	N
A		O
G	E	T

21. FROZEN
22. WINDOWS
23. CROSSWORD
24. TELESCOPE
25. HOSPITAL
26. PQ 27. JK
28. LM 29. SP
30. RT 31. 3621
32. 1655 33. BALE
34. 1238 35. GEM
36. paint 37. train
38. notes 39. heater
40. denture

Paper 14
1. idle 2. stupid
3. hot 4. straight
5. never 6. cattle
7. banquet 8. foliage
9. painter 10. drama
Answers may vary:

11.
F	I	T
A		O
B	A	N

12.
D	I	G
A		O
B	U	D

13.
S	E	W
A		I
P	E	G

14.
F	A	N
A		A
R	I	B

15.
V	A	T
A		O
N	O	W

16. tea 17. sheep
18. poppy 19. ice
20. pillow 21. MP
22. WA 23. NO
24. RS 25. PQ
26. 4352 27. 5244
28. ALE 29. 2743
30. GREEN 31. quad
32. satellite 33. kiwi
34. carrot 35. thunder
36. state 37. race
38. roam 39. click
40. spout

Paper 15
1. whales, sails
2. send, mend
3. stool, cool
4. damp, cramp
5. fickle, sickle
6. diluted 7. off
8. empty 9. gentle
10. night 11. beaker
12. cloak 13. snatch
14. twist 15. slope
Answers may vary:

16.
B	E	D
A		I
N	I	P

17.
S	I	P
O		A
N	O	D

18.
T	I	P
A		I
P	E	N

19.
E	L	F
A		O
R	Y	E

20.
B	O	W
A		I
T	O	N

21. butterfly 22. silver
23. green 24. dictionary
25. weather 26. BIRTHDAY
27. ROCKS 28. YELLOW
29. LIBRARY 30. PEOPLE
31. 4112 32. NEST
33. 1524 34. 4215
35. FREE 36. purse

37. dinner 38. boots
39. wagon 40. valleys

Paper 16
1. skittle, whittle
2. cutter, shutter
3. coat, smote
4. mouse, louse
5. whether, feather
6. enemy 7. empty
8. push 9. common
10. smooth 11. poultry
12. dagger 13. ring
14. exchange 15. slide
16. third 17. wood
18. negative 19. nursery
20. hearts 21. TELEVISION
22. GOLDFISH 23. FOREST
24. SHOPS 25. MOUNTAIN
26. EB 27. RT
28. MNO 29. KZ
30. RI 31. tractor
32. silver 33. potato
34. weight 35. title
36. sweat 37. dreary
38. cheery 39. baker
40. corner

Paper 17
1. craft, draft
2. ashen, fashion
3. bloat, wrote
4. find, bind
5. brighter, mitre
6. pail 7. pony
8. coach 9. captain
10. sum
Answers may vary:

11.
O	W	L
A		A
T	I	P

12.
P	I	N
A		A
D	A	Y

13.
R	Y	E
A		N
P	O	D

14.
S	E	T
A		O
G	I	N

15.
T	A	P
E		I
A	P	E

16. floor 17. small
18. metal 19. princess
20. sewing 21. WAITER
22. EXHAUSTED
23. FRUITS
24. MUSICIANS
25. BISCUIT 26. EJ
27. HU 28. RI
29. MI 30. VTR
31. 1432 32. NOW
33. 57327 34. 3287
35. CAPE 36. saint
37. rotate 38. crease
39. reply 40. invade

3

Paper 18
1. bellow, mellow
2. best, rest
3. mine, whine
4. head, fed
5. brain, reign
6. novice
7. slow
8. conclusion
9. active
10. thin
11. shovel
12. steps
13. money
14. talk
15. divide

Answers may vary:
16.
F	I	N
A	I	
T	O	P

17.
A	M	P
X		I
E	V	E

18.
H	A	Y
A		A
M	O	P

19.
V	A	T
A		R
N	A	Y

20.
Z	I	P
O		I
O	N	E

21. POLISH
22. GARDEN
23. POULTRY
24. HARVEST
25. CHILDREN
26. QR
27. JX
28. IV
29. DX DT
30. EOP
31. house
32. sugar
33. paper
34. stone
35. rafter
36. tense
37. itch
38. indent
39. tanner
40. fed

Paper 19
1. faction, fraction
2. banter, ranter
3. fallow, callow
4. liner, minor
5. crop, flop
6. relaxed
7. from
8. lost
9. stale
10. ugly
11. fluff
12. drive
13. lid
14. jive
15. strike

Answers may vary:
16.
H	I	P
O		I
T	O	E

17.
M	O	P
A		O
D	I	P

18.
F	A	D
E		I
D	O	N

19.
C	A	N
O		O
P	A	R

20.
B	E	E
E		Y
D	O	E

21. sultana
22. fruit
23. cabin
24. pupil
25. money
26. MORNING
27. ILLUSTRATED
28. POTATO
29. MICROSCOPE
30. AUTOGRAPH

31. NX
32. NK
33. MO
34. IG
35. NLK
36. adorn
37. train
38. reef
39. racial
40. path

Paper 20
1. sheep, deep
2. knack, stack
3. might, white
4. mould, bold
5. thank, drank
6. dry
7. export
8. poor
9. hate
10. solidifying

Answers may vary:
11.
T	W	O
I		U
N	O	R

12.
M	E	N
A		A
P	I	P

13.
F	O	G
A		O
R	E	D

14.
W	I	T
A		I
S	A	P

15.
N	I	B
O		I
D	I	D

16. stripes
17. cold
18. cub
19. oak
20. floor
21. BU
22. FK
23. LJ
24. HV
25. QRS
26. 6314
27. 1564
28. BUY
29. 1452
30. SEAS
31. his
32. entry
33. gloves
34. skin
35. chaotic
36. happen
37. fancy
38. greet
39. shuts
40. miners

Paper 21
1. drench, bench
2. game, same
3. talk, chalk
4. rubble, trouble
5. scamper, pamper
6. pluck
7. cease
8. sing
9. coach
10. away

Answers may vary:
11.
P	A	T
O		E
T	A	N

12.
A	L	L
G		I
E	Y	E

13.
D	A	B
O		I
T	U	B

14.
T	O	R
O		U
W	I	G

15.
B	O	W
O		I
Y	E	N

16. hexagon
17. square
18. apple
19. flake
20. hearing
21. VW
22. RO
23. XH
24. CST
25. EJ
26. 1324
27. BYE
28. 14225
29. 2143
30. TART
31. heal
32. bread
33. door
34. palate
35. fulfil
36. wheat
37. habit
38. brace
39. local
40. mean

Paper 22
1. wheel, real
2. frock, wok
3. nit, flit
4. colder, shoulder
5. gave, waive
6. blunt
7. long
8. south
9. find
10. foolish
11. pillow
12. bunch
13. tune
14. ale
15. cost

Answers may vary:
16.
D	E	N
A		O
M	A	T

17.
K	I	P
I		A
D	I	N

18.
W	O	K
A		I
S	A	D

19.
F	E	N
O		O
R	A	T

20.
P	I	N
A		E
W	I	T

21. HELICOPTER
22. ENVELOPE
23. ROCKPOOLS
24. BENEATH
25. FIREWORKS
26. 6536
27. MEN
28. 5211
29. 2321
30. FRAME
31. mosquito
32. garden
33. statue
34. pillow
35. panel
36. purple
37. drear
38. sudden
39. strain
40. corner

PAPER 12

Underline the two words in each set that rhyme with the word in capitals.

Example

CAT　　mate　　<u>mat</u>　　freight　　pant　　<u>sat</u>

1. WAITER　　water　　<u>cater</u>　　canter　　lighter　　<u>later</u>
2. METAL　　pistil　　wattle　　little　　<u>mettle</u>　　<u>petal</u>
3. MINT　　plinth　　<u>flint</u>　　<u>dint</u>　　skein　　feint
4. PLATE　　<u>wait</u>　　palate　　crater　　<u>mate</u>　　faint
5. FROST　　roast　　<u>cost</u>　　ghost　　host　　<u>lost</u>

Which word in each set is opposite in meaning to the word in capitals? Underline the word.

Example

HOT　　steaming　　warm　　frozen　　<u>cold</u>

6. ROUGH　　uneven　　bumpy　　<u>smooth</u>　　coarse
7. SHOUT　　yell　　<u>whisper</u>　　talk　　sing
8. SUMMER　　autumn　　season　　<u>winter</u>　　spring
9. TRUE　　promise　　oath　　statement　　<u>false</u>
10. WILD　　danger　　<u>tame</u>　　natural　　escaped

Which word in each set is most similar in meaning to the word in capitals? Underline the word.

Example

FAST　　hurry　　slow　　<u>quick</u>　　race

11. CRY　　tears　　hankie　　<u>sob</u>　　sad
12. QUESTION　　answer　　know　　lesson　　<u>ask</u>

Paper 12

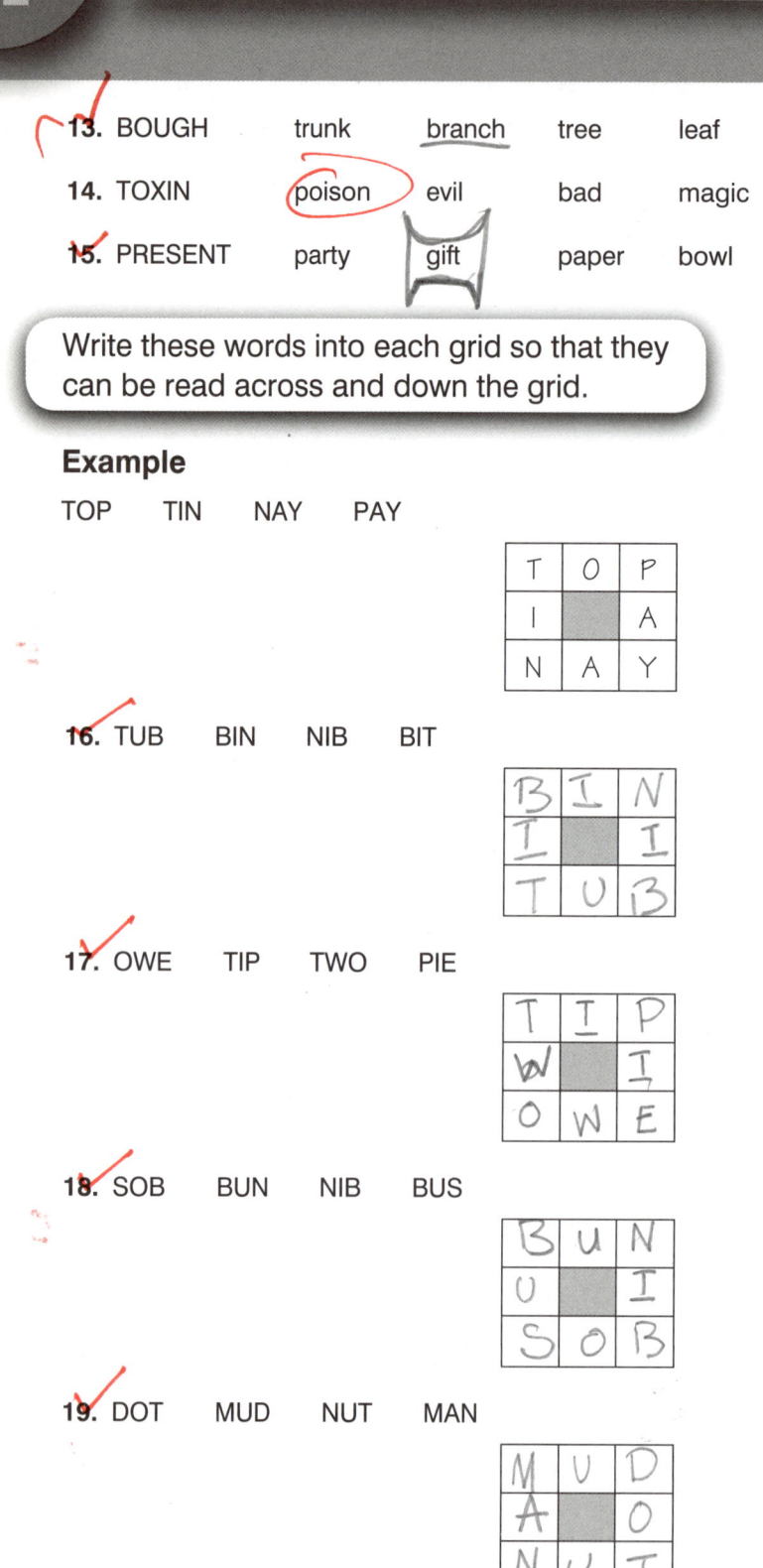

13. BOUGH   trunk   <u>branch</u>   tree   leaf
14. TOXIN   (poison)   evil   bad   magic
15. PRESENT   party   gift   paper   bowl

4/5

Write these words into each grid so that they can be read across and down the grid.

Example
TOP   TIN   NAY   PAY

T	O	P
I		A
N	A	Y

16. TUB   BIN   NIB   BIT

B	I	N
I		I
T	U	B

17. OWE   TIP   TWO   PIE

T	I	P
W		I
O	W	E

18. SOB   BUN   NIB   BUS

B	U	N
U		I
S	O	B

19. DOT   MUD   NUT   MAN

M	U	D
A		O
N	U	T

48

20. RAT   CUB   CAR   BAT

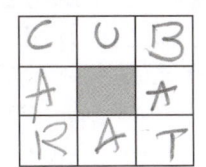

C	U	B
A		A
R	A	T

5/5

In each sentence below, rearrange the word in capitals to make a properly spelt word that completes the sentence. Write the word on the answer line.

Example

The children were late for SLOHOC.   <u>SCHOOL</u>

21. The children played PKPINSIG games in the playground. <u>SKIPPING</u>
22. There was an ornamental NTANOFUI in the middle of the garden. <u>FOUNTAIN</u>
23. His team had a great RYCTIVO at the weekend. <u>VICTORY</u>
24. The children were growing ETABEGLEVS at school. <u>VEGETABLES</u>
25. He prepared a fantastic poster on the MTCPUERO. <u>COMPUTER</u>

4/5

Look carefully at the given codes and work out the answers to the questions.

Example

If the code for SEAM is 3415, what does the code 341 stand for?   <u>SEA</u>

If the code for RAFTS is 45213:

26. What is the code for STAR? <u>3154</u>
27. What is the code for TART? <u>1541</u>
28. What does the code 31522 stand for? <u>STAFF</u>

If the code for STALE is 67924:

29. What is the code for TELL? <u>7422</u>
30. What does the code 6297 stand for? <u>SLAT</u>

5/5

49

Paper 12

Underline the odd word out in each of these sets.
(Look carefully at the spelling **or** meaning of each word.)

Example

spring   <u>flung</u>   fling   string

31. bounce   flounce   ounce   <u>courage</u>

32. dolly   <u>valley</u>   holly   folly

33. <u>yard</u>   mile   inch   ounce

34. girl   sister   <u>uncle</u>   mother

35. dinner   lunch   <u>menu</u>   breakfast

4/5

Which word in each set **cannot** be made using the letters of the word in capitals? Underline the word.

Example

PLATE   tea   tape   leap   <u>pail</u>

36. DINOSAUR   sand   <u>nose</u>   rind   around

37. EMERALD   male   deer   dame   <u>land</u>

38. FLAMES   meal   <u>miles</u>   safe   slam

39. GLOBAL   ball   goal   gall   <u>local</u>

40. HARMFUL   farm   <u>hall</u>   haul   maul

5/5

31/40

PAPER 13

Underline the two words in each set that rhyme with the word in capitals.

Example
CAT   mate   mat   freight   pant   sat

1. PRISON   risen   hidden   prize   visitor   wizen
2. REASON   treason   caution   season   sensation   weasel
3. MASTER   castor   charger   plaster   waster   traitor
4. CROP   drop   frock   shop   croup   chomp
5. FLIGHT   white   spine   flint   height   freight

5/5

Which word in each set is opposite in meaning to the word in capitals? Underline the word.

Example
HOT   steaming   warm   frozen   cold

6. ANCIENT   old   original   modern   antique
7. BLACK   grey   white   colour   dark
8. DOMESTIC   cultivated   rare   tamed   wild
9. DULL   clean   shiny   dirty   cloudy
10. EAST   north   direction   south   west

4/5

Which word in each set is most similar in meaning to the word in capitals? Underline the word.

Example
FAST   hurry   slow   quick   race

11. SOUP   broth   supper   bread   hot
12. STALE   bread   mouldy   old   fresh

51

Paper 13

13. PONDER   ask   <u>think</u>   decide   gaze

14. SEARCH   lose   treasure   find   <u>seek</u>

15. SHOCK   power   wave   <u>fright</u>   jump

5/5

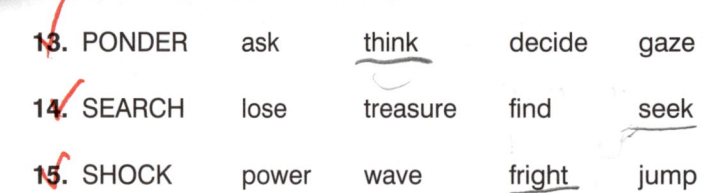

> Write these words into each grid so that they can be read across and down the grid.

Example

TOP   TIN   NAY   PAY

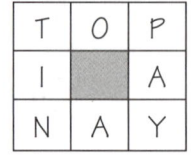

T	O	P
I		A
N	A	Y

16. WIT   NOW   LOT   NIL

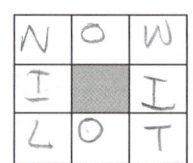

N	O	W
I		I
L	O	T

17. NOT   OWN   ORE   EAT

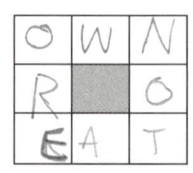

O	W	N
R		O
E	A	T

18. HEM   HIT   TOW   MOW

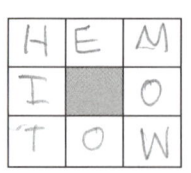

H	E	M
I		O
T	O	W

19. WET   ROW   RIG   GET

R	O	W
I		E
G	E	T

52

Paper 13

20. NAG   NOT   NUN   GET

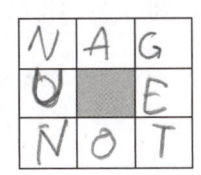

|N|A|G|
|U| |E|
|N|O|T|

5/5

In each sentence below, rearrange the word in capitals to make a properly spelt word that completes the sentence. Write the word on the answer line.

Example

The children were late for SLOHOC.   SCHOOL

21. The pond was RNFOZE over all winter. FROZEN

22. The curtains were drawn across the DONWISW. WINDOWS

23. She loved doing the SWORROCSD puzzle each day. CROSSWORD

24. Grandfather gazed at the stars through his TEPSCOELE. TELESCOPE

25. He was rushed to the THLPIAOS after the accident. HOSPITAL

4/5

Look carefully at these letter sequences. Work out the patterns to find the next letters in each sequence. The alphabet is here to help you.

A B C D E F G H I J K L M N O P Q R S T U V W X Y Z

Example

AB   DE   GH   JK   ?   MN

26. LM   KJ   NO   IH   PQ   GF

27. AD   BC   EH   FG   IL   JK

28. XY   UV   RS   OP   LM

29. SR   ST   SQ   SU   SP   SV

30. BD   FH   JL   NP   RT

5/5

53

Paper 13

Look carefully at the given codes and work out the answers to the questions.

Example

If the code for SEAM is 3415, what does the code 341 stand for?   SEA

If the code for TABLE is 12356:

31. What is the code for BEAT? 3621
32. What is the code for TELL? 1655
33. What does the code 3256 stand for? BALE

If the code for MERGE is 82312:

34. What is the code for GERM? 1238
35. What does the code 128 stand for? GEM

3/5

Underline the odd word out in each of these sets.
(Look carefully at the spelling **or** meaning of each word.)

Example

spring   <u>flung</u>   fling   string

36. brown   red   <u>paint</u>   purple
37. car   <u>train</u> lorry   bus
38. violin   flute   piano   <u>notes</u>
39. feather   heather   <u>heater</u> weather
40. donate   <u>denture</u> donation donated

5/5

37/40

PAPER 14

Which word on the right is opposite in meaning to the word in capitals on the left? Underline the word.

Example

HOT   steaming   warm   frozen   <u>cold</u>

1. BUSY   rushing   chaos   <u>idle</u>   time
2. CLEVER   intelligent   student   nonsense   <u>stupid</u>
3. COLD   warm   <u>hot</u>   boiling   freezing
4. CURLY   frizzy   wavy   <u>straight</u>   long
5. ALWAYS   often   <u>never</u>   frequency   occasional

5/5

Which word in each set is most similar in meaning to the word in capitals? Underline the word.

Example

FAST   hurry   slow   <u>quick</u>   race

6. COWS   <u>cattle</u>   herd   milk   calves
7. FEAST   famine   dinner   bake   <u>banquet</u>
8. LEAVES   bud   roots   <u>foliage</u>   forest
9. ARTIST   colours   easel   <u>painter</u>   brush
10. PLAY   programme   <u>drama</u>   actor   theatre

5/5

Write these words into the grid so that they can be read across and down the grid.

Example

TOP   TIN   NAY   PAY

T	O	P
I		A
N	A	Y

11. BAN   TON   FAB   FIT

F	A	B
I		A
T	O	N

12. GOD   DIG   BUD   DAB

D	I	G
A		O
B	U	D

13. SEW   PEG   SAP   WIG

S	E	W
A		I
P	E	G

14. FAR   NAB   FAN   RIB

F	A	R
A		I
N	A	B

15. VAN   NOW   VAT   TOW

V	A	N
A		O
T	O	W

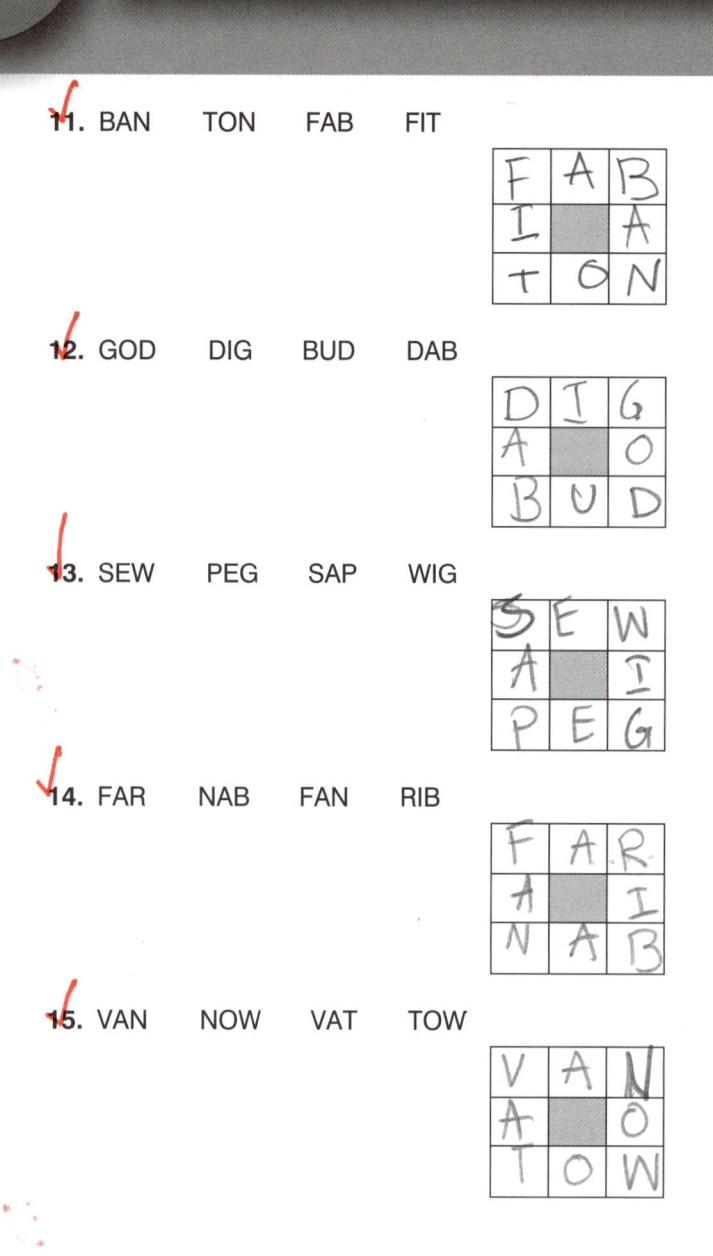

Underline the word in the brackets that completes the second pair of words in the same way as the first pair.

Example

A is to B as one is to (to, <u>two</u>, too, three).

16. Bean is to coffee as leaf is to (cup, kettle, pot, <u>tea</u>).

17. Beef is to cow as mutton is to (chop, <u>sheep</u>, wool, flock).

Paper 14

18. Yellow is to daffodil as red is to (snowdrop, bluebell, apple, poppy).

19. Ski is to snow as skate is to (rink, ice, blade, speed).

20. Chair is to cushion as bed is to (duvet, sleep, night, pillow).

5/5

Look carefully at these letter sequences. Work out the patterns to find the next letters in each sequence. The alphabet is here to help you.

A B C D E F G H I J K L M N O P Q R S T U V W X Y Z

Example

AB   DE   GH   JK   ?   MN

21. PS   OR   NQ   MP   LO

22. ZD   YC   XB   WA   VZ

23. BC   FE   HI   LK   NO

24. HI   JL   MN   OQ   RS   TV

25. AB   DE   GH   JK   MN   PQ

/5

Look carefully at the given codes and work out the answers to the questions.

Example

If the code for STEAM is 32415, what does the code 341 stand for?   SEA

If the codes for ALL and TEA are 344 and 523:

26. What is the code for LATE?   4352

27. What is the code for TELL?   5244

28. What does the code 342 stand for?   ALE

If the code for ANGER is 74312:

29. What is the code for RANG? __2743__

30. What does the code 32114 stand for? __GREEN__

Underline the odd word out in each of these sets.
(Look carefully at the spelling **or** the meaning of each word.)

Example
spring   <u>flung</u>   fling   string

31. couple   twin   duet   <u>quad</u>

32. star   <u>satellite</u>   planet   meteor

33. raspberry   strawberry   cherry   <u>kiwi</u>

34. <u>carrot</u>   cabbage   lettuce   spinach

35. fog   mist   cloud   <u>thunder</u>

Which words in each set **cannot** be made using the letters of the word in capitals? Underline the word.

Example
PLATE   tea   tape   leap   <u>pail</u>

36. INSTANT   state   stain   taints   <u>saint</u>

37. LECTURE   cure   cuter   <u>race</u>   true

38. MEASURE   same   reams   amuse   <u>roam</u>

39. NECKLACE   lack   cackle   <u>click</u>   kale

40. OPPOSITE   spite   <u>spout</u>   poise   stop

PAPER 15

Underline the two words in each set that rhyme with the word in capitals.

Example

CAT   <u>mate</u>   mat   freight   pant   <u>sat</u>

1. SCALES   calls   <u>whales</u>   seals   silos   <u>sails</u>
2. BEND   wind   <u>send</u>   melt   <u>mend</u>   wand
3. POOL   stoop   loop   <u>stool</u>   cool   sour
4. STAMP   <u>damp</u>   camper   limp   <u>cramp</u>   stomp
5. PICKLE   <u>fickle</u>   fiddle   <u>peck</u>   sickle   cycle

5/5

Which word in each set is opposite in meaning to the word in capitals? Underline the word.

Example

HOT   steaming   warm   frozen   <u>cold</u>

6. CONCENTRATED   strong   solution   <u>diluted</u>   sharp
7. ON   of   <u>off</u>   over   under
8. CROWDED   mass   silent   <u>empty</u>   throng
9. FIERCE   hunter   <u>gentle</u>   wild   dangerous
10. DAY   dark   stars   sheep   <u>night</u>

5/5

Which word on the right is most similar in meaning to the word in capitals on the left? Underline the word.

Example

FAST   hurry   slow   <u>quick</u>   race

11. TUMBLER   bottle   jug   pot   <u>beaker</u>
12. CAPE   cardigan   <u>cloak</u>   dress   scarf

13. GRAB   snatch   take   request   borrow
14. TURN   over   undo   twist   close
15. INCLINE   mountain   brakes   slope   ground

5/5

Write these words into each grid so that they can be read across and down the grid.

Example
TOP   TIN   NAY   PAY

T	O	P
I		A
N	A	Y

16. NIP   BED   BAN   DIP

B	E	D
A		I
N	I	P

17. PAD   SON   SIP   NOD

S	O	N
I		O
P	A	D

18. PIN   TIP   TAP   PEN

T	I	P
A		E
P	I	N

19. ELF   RYE   EAR   FOE

E	A	R
L		Y
F	O	E

20. BOW   BAT   TON   WIN

|B|O|W|
|A| |I|
|T|O|N|

5/5

> Underline the word in the brackets that completes the second pair of words in the same way as the first pair.

Example
A is to B as one is to (to, <u>two</u>, too, three).

21. Tadpole is to frog as caterpillar is to (eggs, chrysalis, metamorphosis, <u>butterfly</u>).

22. First is to gold, as second is to (place, medal, bronze, <u>silver</u>).

23. Ruby is to red as emerald is to (shamrock, Ireland, <u>green</u>, stone).

24. Directions is to map as spelling is to (recipe, encyclopaedia, <u>dictionary</u>, directions).

25. Geology is to rocks as meteorology is to (space, planes, storms, <u>weather</u>).

5/5

> In each sentence below, rearrange the word in capitals to make a properly spelt word that completes the sentence. Write the word on the answer line.

Example
The children were late for SLOHOC.   <u>SCHOOL</u>

26. Tom was very excited the day before his DATHIBRY. <u>BIRTHDay</u>

27. During the storm, the waves were crashing against the CROSK. <u>ROCKS</u>

28. The old lady had a bright LYLOWE parrot. <u>YELLOW</u>

29. There were lots of people in the BRAIRLY enjoying the new books. <u>LIBRARY</u>

30. The annual show attracted lots of LEOPPE to the village. <u>PEOPLE</u>

5/5

Paper 15

Look carefully at the codes and work out the answers to the questions.

Example

If the code for SEAM is 3415, what does the code 341 stand for?   SEA

If the code for TENTS is 31234: *(31234)*

31. What is the code for SEEN? 4112
32. What does the code 2143 stand for? NEST

If the code for FARMER is 321451: *(321451)*

33. What is the code for REAM? 1524
34. What is the code for MARE? 4215
35. What does the code 3155 stand for? FREE

Underline the odd word out in each of these sets.
(Look carefully at the spelling **or** meaning of each word.)

Example

spring   <u>flung</u>   fling   string

36. money   <u>notes</u>   coins   purse
37. peas   cabbage   <u>dinner</u>   carrot
38. hat   <u>boots</u>   helmet   beret
39. platoon   pontoon   <u>wagon</u>   lagoon
40. babies   ladies   pennies   <u>valleys</u>

5/5

5/5

40/40

PAPER 16

Underline the two words in each set that rhyme with the word in capitals.

Example

CAT　　mate　　<u>mat</u>　　freight　　pant　　<u>sat</u>

1. BRITTLE　　billet　　<u>skittle</u>　　title　　nettle　　<u>whittle</u>
2. BUTTER　　hunter　　<u>cutter</u>　　cuter　　duster　　<u>shutter</u>
3. FLOAT　　bloated　　<u>coat</u>　　great　　<u>smote</u>　　moult
4. HOUSE　　chose　　<u>mouse</u>　　coarse　　horse　　<u>louse</u>
5. WEATHER　　hearth　　merger　　<u>whether</u>　　<u>feather</u>　　father

4 /5

Which word in each set is opposite in meaning to the word in capitals? Underline the word.

Example

HOT　　steaming　　warm　　frozen　　<u>cold</u>

6. FRIEND　　follower　　mate　　<u>enemy</u>　　student
7. FULL　　capacity　　level　　<u>empty</u>　　flowing
8. PULL　　yank　　<u>push</u>　　take　　thrust
9. RARE　　unusual　　special　　individual　　<u>common</u>
10. WRINKLED　　bumpy　　creased　　<u>smooth</u>　　slimy

5 /5

Which word in each set is most similar in meaning to the word in capitals? Underline the word.

Example

FAST　　hurry　　slow　　<u>quick</u>　　race

11. CHICKEN　　pie　　drumstick　　roast　　<u>poultry</u>
12. KNIFE　　cut　　danger　　threaten　　<u>dagger</u>

Paper 16

13. CHIME	ring	bell	tower	rope
14. SWAP	give	exchange	take	ask
15. SLIP	slide	tumble	break	lose

5/5

Underline the word in the brackets that completes the second pair of words in the same way as the first pair.

Example

A is to B as one is to (to, <u>two</u>, too, three).

16. Gold is to first as bronze is to (fourth, second, <u>third</u>, badge).
17. Blacksmith is to metal as carpenter is to (hammer, <u>wood</u>, saw, chisel).
18. Plus is to minus as positive is to (hopeful, adding, <u>negative</u>, subtracting).
19. Children is to school as baby is to (crying, sleeping, cot, <u>nursery</u>).
20. Spades is to clubs, as diamonds is to (cards, <u>hearts</u>, red, ace).

5/5

In each sentence below, rearrange the word in capitals to make a properly spelt word that completes the sentences. Write the word on the answer line.

Example

The children were late for SLOHOC.   <u>SCHOOL</u>

21. It was their favourite VISITOELEN programme. <u>TELEVISION</u>
22. There were lots of SDFIOGLH in the pond. <u>GOLD Fish</u>
23. He ran into the EFTSOR and had a rest under the trees. <u>FOREST</u>
24. The HOSSP were very crowded. <u>SHOPS</u>
25. They flew over the famous ONUNTAMI range. <u>MOUNTAIN</u>

5/5

Paper 16

Look carefully at these letter sequences. Work out the patterns to find the next letters in each sequence. The alphabet is here to help you.

A B C D E F G H I J K L M N O P Q R S T U V W X Y Z

Example

AB   DE   GH   JK   ?   MN

26. AX   BY   CZ   DA   EB
27. FH   IK   LN   OQ   RT
28. ABC FED GHI LKJ MNO
29. HW   IX   JY   KZ   LA
30. ZA   XC   VE   TG   RI

/5

Underline the odd word out in each of these sets.
(Look carefully at the spelling **or** meaning of each word.)

Example

spring   <u>flung</u>   fling   string

31. orchard   forest   meadow   <u>tractor</u>
32. sparkly   silver   shiny   silvery
33. grape   raisin   <u>potato</u>   sultana
34. science   fiend   <u>weight</u>   friend
35. middle   bubble   goggle   title

/5

Which of the words in each set **cannot** be made using the letters of the word in capitals? Underline the word.

Example

PLATE   tea   tape   leap   <u>pail</u>

36. WEASEL   laws   sale   <u>sweat</u>   sew
37. YESTERDAY   drey   <u>dreary</u>   tray   yards
38. ARCHERY   reach   cheery   acre   racer
39. BLANKET   bank   table   <u>baker</u>   able
40. CROWNED   crowed   <u>corner</u>   rowed   word

/5

39/40

65

PAPER 17

Underline the two words in each set that rhyme with the word in capitals.

Example
CAT   mate   <u>mat</u>   freight   pant   <u>sat</u>

1. AFT   <u>craft</u>   sift   waft   drift   <u>draft</u>
2. PASSION   pattern   vision   ashen   <u>fashion</u>   <u>mission</u>
3. COAT   <u>bloat</u>   cool   <u>wrote</u>   moult   coot
4. KIND   <u>find</u>   <u>bind</u>   lint   kink   think
5. WRITER   <u>brighter</u>   centre   mitre   <u>mister</u>   welter

5/5

Which word in each set is most similar in meaning to the word in capitals? Underline the word.

Example
FAST   hurry   slow   <u>quick</u>   race

6. BUCKET   water   handle   <u>pail</u>   plastic
7. HORSE   saddle   riding   reins   <u>pony</u>
8. BUS   car   bicycle   <u>coach</u>   van
9. LEADER   team   <u>captain</u>   win   party
10. TOTAL   <u>sum</u>   multiply   add   subtract

5/5

Write these words into the grid so that they can be read across and down the grid.

Example
TOP   TIN   NAY   PAY

T	O	P
I		A
N	A	Y

11. TIP   OAT   OWL   LAP

|O|A|T|
|W| |I|
|L|A|P|

12. NAY   DAY   PAD   PIN

|P|A|D|
|I| |A|
|N|A|Y|

13. POD   RYE   END   RAP

|R|Y|E|
|A| |N|
|P|O|D|

14. TON   SET   SAG   GIN

|S|E|T|
|A| |O|
|G|I|N|

15. PIE   APE   TEA   TAP

|T|E|A|
|A| |P|
|D|I|E|

5 /5

Underline the word in the brackets that completes the second pair of words in the same way as the first pair.

Example
A is to B as one is to (to, <u>two</u>, too, three).

16. Roof is to ground as ceiling is to (cellar, building, tiles, <u>floor</u>).

17. Elephant is to large as mouse is to (mammal, cheese, <u>small</u>, squeak).

Paper 17

18. Granite is to stone as copper is to (coins, pennies, mineral, metal).

19. King is to queen as prince is to (countess, duchess, princess, lady).

20. Pen is to writing as needle is to (cotton, sewing, stitches, embroidery).

5/5

> In each sentence below, rearrange the word in capitals to make a properly spelt word that completes the sentences. Write the word on the answer line.

Example

The children were late for SLOHOC.   SCHOOL

21. The AIERTW brought them each a menu. **WAITER**

22. The runners were EUSTEXHAD because of the heat. **EXHAUSTED**

23. On holiday, they tried lots of the unusual RUTIFS and vegetables. **FRUITS**

24. The ANMCIUSIS rehearsed for hours before the concert. **MUSICIANS**

25. She helped herself to another chocolate BUTICIS. **BISCUIT**

5/5

> Look carefully at these letter sequences. Work out the patterns to find the next letters in each sequence. The alphabet is here to help you.

A B C D E F G H I J K L M N O P Q R S T U V W X Y Z

Example

AB   DE   GH   JK   ?   MN

26. AF   BG   CH   DI   **EJ**

27. LQ   KR   JS   IT   **HU**

28. VE   FU   TG   HS   **RI**

29. KE   KF   LG   LH   **MI**   MJ

30. ZXV   YWU   XVT   WUS   **VTR**   USQ

5/5

68

Paper 17

Look carefully at the given codes and work out the answers to the questions.

Example

If the code for SEAM is 3415, what does the code 341 stand for?   SEA

If the code for CROWN is 63412: *(63412 written above)*

31. What is the code for WORN? __1432__

32. What does the code 241 stand for? __NOW__

If the code for CHEAP is 28735: *(28735 written above)*

33. What is the code for PEACE? __57327__

34. What is the code for ACHE? __3287__

35. What does the code 2357 stand for? __CAPE__

5/5

Which of the words in each set **cannot** be made using the letters of the word in capitals? Underline the word.

Example
PLATE   tea   tape   leap   <u>pail</u>

36. PLEASANT   leaps   <u>saint</u>   seal   plate

37. ROTARY   tarry   try   <u>tray</u>   rotate

38. STAIRCASE   <u>crease</u>   casters   asset   crate

39. TRIPLE   ripe   tripe   <u>reply</u>   lip

40. VALIDATE   vale   lived   alive   <u>invade</u>

5/5

39/40

PAPER 18

Underline the two words in each set that rhyme with the word in capitals.

Example

CAT   mate   <u>mat</u>   freight   pant   <u>sat</u>

1. YELLOW   <u>bellow</u>   below   hollow   <u>mellow</u>   sorrel
2. WEST   feast   <u>best</u>   mast   <u>rest</u>   least
3. VINE   <u>mine</u>   minor   vein   <u>whine</u>   rhyme
4. BREAD   <u>head</u>   bead   fed   <u>bleed</u>   bean
5. CRANE   tame   <u>brain</u>   groan   paid   <u>reign</u>

4/5

Which word in each set is opposite in meaning to the word in capitals? Underline the word.

Example

HOT   steaming   warm   frozen   <u>cold</u>

6. EXPERT   professional   <u>novice</u>   child   leader
7. FAST   quick   rush   creep   <u>slow</u>
8. INTRODUCTION   opening   <u>conclusion</u>   preface   plot
9. LAZY   idle   <u>active</u>   sleepy   dozy
10. FAT   plump   narrow   wide   <u>thin</u>

5/5

Which word in each set is most similar in meaning to the word in capitals? Underline the word.

Example

FAST   hurry   slow   <u>quick</u>   race

11. SPADE   <u>shovel</u>   fork   hoe   rake
12. LADDER   fall   height   move   <u>steps</u>

13. CASH   cost   supply   money   purse
14. CHAT   question talk   integrate sing
15. SHARE   give   take   divide   cut

5/5

Write these words into each grid so that they can be read across and down the grid.

Example
TOP   TIN   NAY   PAY

T	O	P
I		A
N	A	Y

16. NIP   FIN   TOP   FAT

F	I	N
A		I
T	O	P

17. AXE   EVE   PIE   AMP

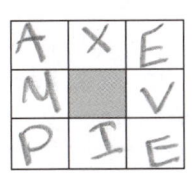

A	X	E
M		V
P	I	E

18. YAP   HAM   MOP   HAY

H	A	M
A		O
Y	A	P

19. NAY   VAN   TRY   VAT

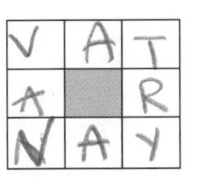

V	A	T
A		R
N	A	Y

Paper 18

20. ZIP   PIE   ONE   ZOO

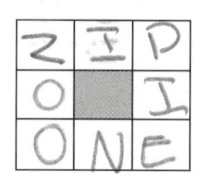

```
Z I P
O   I
O N E
```

5/5

In each sentence below, rearrange the word in capitals to make a properly spelt word that completes the sentences. Write the word on the answer line.

Example

The children were late for SLOHOC.   SCHOOL

21. After a good ISPLHO, the candlestick shone. POLISH
22. The wet dogs raced around the ARENDG. GARDEN
23. The farm kept TROPLUY and pigs. POULTRY
24. The men worked hard to finish the ARHSVET before the storm. HARVEST
25. The NHILRECD played with their new computer games. CHILDREN

5/5

Look carefully at these letter sequences. Work out the patterns to find the next letters in each sequence. The alphabet is here to help you.

A B C D E F G H I J K L M N O P Q R S T U V W X Y Z

Example

AB   DE   GH   JK   ?   MN

26. EF   HI   KL   NO   QR
27. BT   DU   FV   HW   JX
28. MZ   LY   KX   JW   DX   IV

29. FZ   FX   EY   EW   IV   DV
30. AKL   BLM   CMN   DNO   EOP

3/5

Underline the odd word out in each of these sets.
(Look carefully at the spelling **or** meaning of each word.)

Example
spring   <u>flung</u>   fling   string

31. house   table   chair   bed
32. orange   green   pink   <u>sugar</u>
33. bronze   silver   <u>paper</u>   gold
34. strong   <u>stone</u>   street   stripe
35. wrapper   write   <u>rafter</u>   wreck

5/5

Which of the words in each set **cannot** be made using the letters of the word in capitals? Underline the word.

Example
PLATE   tea   tape   leap   <u>pail</u>

36. KITTENS   kites   inset   <u>tense</u>   tents
37. LICHEN   chin   <u>itch</u>   inch   lice
38. MINTED   dine   edit   <u>indent</u>   dent
39. NEATEN   eaten   ante   <u>tanner</u>   ate
40. TOFFEE   toe   oft   fee   <u>fed</u>

5/5

37/40

PAPER 19

Underline the two words in each set that rhyme with the word in capitals.

Example

CAT   mate   <u>mat</u>   freight   pant   <u>sat</u>

1. ACTION   station   <u>faction</u>   <u>fraction</u>   mention   notion
2. CANTER   panther   <u>banter</u>   bantam   <u>ranter</u>   centre
3. SHALLOW   morrow   wallow   <u>fallow</u>   <u>callow</u>   hollow
4. MINER   dinner   whine   thinner   <u>liner</u>   <u>minor</u>
5. CHOP   <u>crop</u>   romp   chap   chip   <u>flop</u>

5/5

Which word in each set is opposite in meaning to the word in capitals? Underline the word.

Example

HOT   steaming   warm   frozen   <u>cold</u>

6. TENSE   worried   <u>relaxed</u>   lazy   cautious
7. TO   where   by   at   <u>from</u>
8. FOUND   labelled   find   <u>lost</u>   keep
9. FRESH   new   ancient   <u>stale</u>   dry
10. PRETTY   beautiful   <u>ugly</u>   unusual   old

5/5

Which word in each set is most similar in meaning to the word in capitals? Underline the word.

Example

FAST   hurry   slow   <u>quick</u>   race

11. DOWN   twill   warm   <u>fluff</u>   goose
12. STEER   <u>drive</u>   map   plan   direction

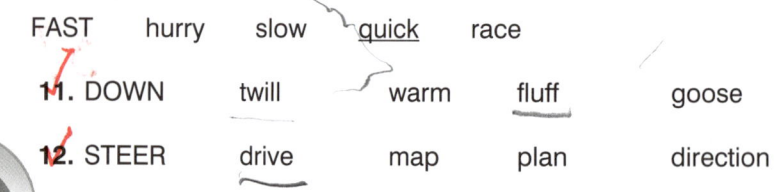

13. TOP   secure   lid   fasten   seal
14. DANCE   music   shoes   jive   ball
15. HIT   bruise   strike   violent   rough

5 /5

Write these words into each grid so that they can be read across and down the grid.

Example

TOP   TIN   NAY   PAY

T	O	P
I		A
N	A	Y

16. TOE   PIE   HIP   HOT

H	I	P
O		I
T	O	E

17. POP   DIP   MAD   MOP

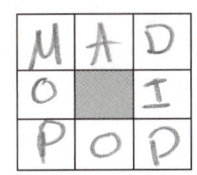

M	A	D
O		I
P	O	P

18. FAD   FED   DIN   DON

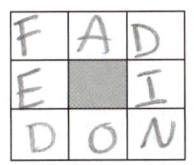

F	A	D
E		I
D	O	N

19. NOR   COP   CAN   PAR

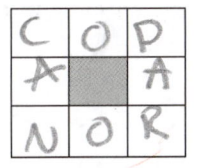

C	O	P
A		A
N	O	R

20. EYE   BED   DOE   BEE

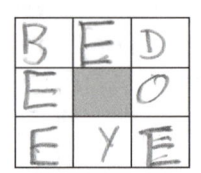

B	E	D
E		O
E	Y	E

Underline the word in the brackets that completes the second pair of words in the same way as the first pair.

Example

A is to B as one is to (to, <u>two</u>, too, three).

21. Plum is to prune as grape is to (wine, juice, <u>sultana</u>, vineyard).

22. Cabbage is to vegetable as apple is to (pie, blossom, pie, <u>fruit</u>, red).

23. Train is to coach as ship is to (rudder, funnel, <u>cabin</u>, cruise).

24. University is to student as school is to (lessons, uniform, <u>pupil</u>, work).

25. Briefcase is to papers as purse is to (shopping, bag, <u>money</u>, key).

In each sentence below, rearrange the word in capitals to make a properly spelt word that completes the sentences. Write the word on the answer line.

Example

The children were late for SLOHOC.   <u>SCHOOL</u>

26. The alarm went early in the RNIONMG. <u>MORNING</u>

27. The children IRATELUSTLD their stories carefully. <u>ILLUSTRATED</u>

28. They had OTPATO chips with their salad. <u>POTATO</u>

29. They looked at the cells through the CPOSCIREMO. <u>MICROSCOPE</u>

30. They asked the famous film star for his APAOHGRUT. <u>AUTOGRAPH</u>

Paper 19

Look carefully at these letter sequences. Work out the patterns to find the next letters in each sequence. The alphabet is here to help you.

A B C D E F G H I J K L M N O P Q R S T U V W X Y Z

Example

AB   DE   GH   JK   ?   <u>MN</u>

31. RT   QU   PV   OW   <u>NX</u>
32. JG   KH   LI   MJ   <u>NK</u>
33. AC   DF   GI   JL   <u>MO</u>
34. YW   US   QO   MK   <u>IG</u>
35. JHG   KIH   LJI   MKJ   <u>NLK</u>

5/5

Which word in each set **cannot** be made using the letters of the word in capitals? Underline your answer.

Example

PLATE   tea   tape   leap   <u>pail</u>

36. DONATION   onion   <u>adorn</u>   nation   noon
37. ENTRANCE   <u>train</u>   create   trace   canter
38. FANFARE   fare   <u>reef</u>   fear   near
39. GLACIER   crag   <u>racial</u>   rage   regal
40. HAPPILY   play   hail   apply   <u>path</u>

5/5

40/40

PAPER 20

Underline the two words in each set that rhyme with the word in capitals.

Example

CAT   mate   <u>mat</u>   freight   pant   <u>sat</u>

1. STEEP   <u>sheep</u>   meat   grief   <u>deep</u>   pleat
2. BLACK   <u>knack</u>   frock   pink   <u>stack</u>   tank
3. KITE   weight   <u>might</u>   print   kind   <u>white</u>
4. FOLD   <u>mould</u>   older   colder   <u>bold</u>   shudder
5. BANK   <u>drink</u>   <u>thank</u>   leant   <u>drank</u>   rink

5/5

Which word in each set is opposite in meaning to the word in capitals on the left. Underline the word.

Example

HOT   steaming   warm   frozen   <u>cold</u>

6. WET   damp   water   heat   <u>dry</u>
7. IMPORT   buy   goods   <u>export</u>   sell
8. RICH   luxury   <u>poor</u>   poverty   workers
9. LOVE   like   dislike   have   <u>hate</u>
10. MELTING   <u>solidifying</u>   saturation   moulting   dissolving

5/5

Write these words into each grid so that they can be read across and down the grid.

Example

TOP   TIN   NAY   PAY

T	O	P
I		A
N	A	Y

11. TIN   NOR   OUR   TWO

T	I	N
W		O
O	U	R

12. MAP   PIP   MEN   NAP

M	A	P
E		I
N	A	P

13. FOG   GOD   RED   FAR

F	O	G
A		O
R	E	D

14. TIP   WAS   SAP   WIT

W	A	S
I		A
T	I	P

15. DID   NIB   BID   NOD

N	I	B
O		I
D	I	D

5/5

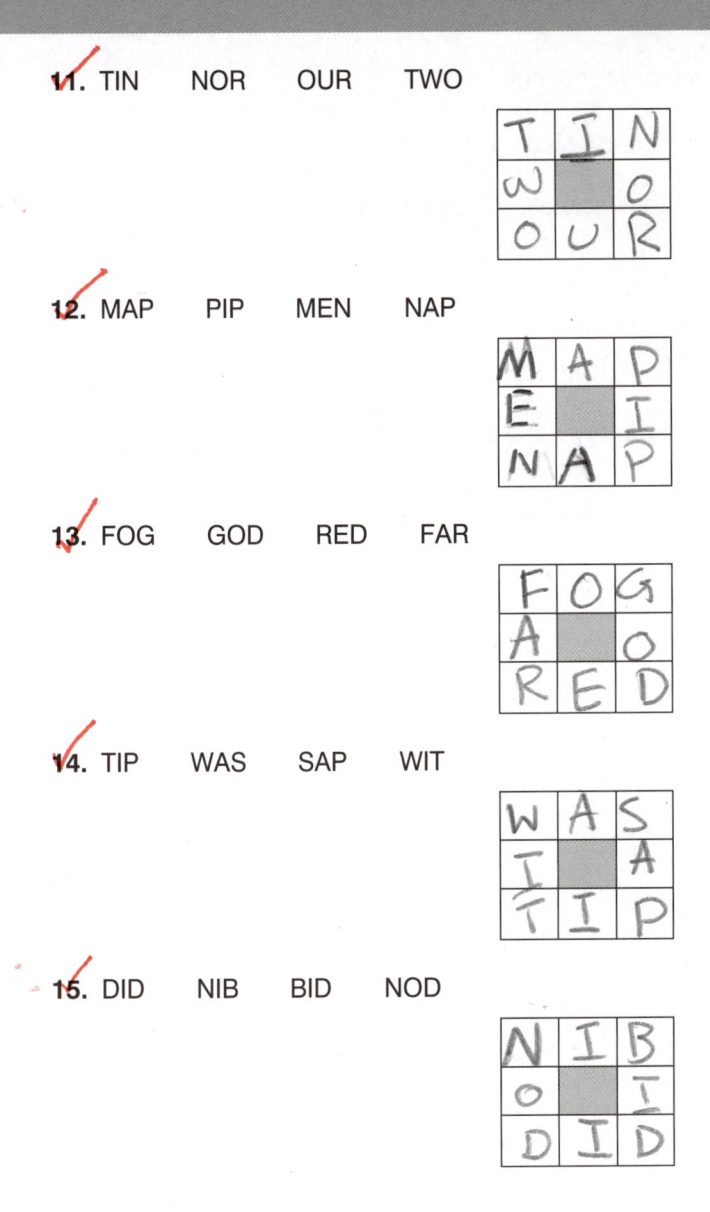

Underline the word in the brackets that completes the second pair of words in the same way as the first pair.

Example

A is to B as one is to (to, <u>two</u>, too, three).

16. Leopard is to spots as tiger is to (danger, claws, <u>stripes</u>, camouflage).

17. Green is to envy as blue is to (sky, healthy, old, <u>cold</u>).

Paper 20

18. Dog is to puppy as lion is to (kitten, young, cub, calf).

19. Seed is to sunflower as acorn is to (tree, plant, oak, forest).

20. Curtain is to window as carpet is to (tiles, colour, hoover, floor).

5/5

Look carefully at these letter sequences. Work out the patterns to find the next letters in each sequence. The alphabet is here to help you.

A B C D E F G H I J K L M N O P Q R S T U V W X Y Z

Example

AB   DE   GH   JK   ?   MN

21. FC   EA   DY   CW   __BU__

22. BG   CH   DI   EJ   __FK__

23. XV   US   RP   OM   __LJ__

24. PZ   NY   LX   JW   __HV__

25. EFG   JIH   KLM   PON   __QRS__

5/5

Look carefully at the given codes and work out the answers to the questions.

Example

If the code for SEAM is 3415, what does the code 341 stand for?   SEA

If the code for BEAUTY is 142365:

26. What is the code for TUBE? __6314__

27. What is the code for BYTE? __1564__

28. What does the code 135 stand for? __BUY__

If the code for SPEAR is 52341:

29. What is the code for RASP? __1452__

30. What does the code 5345 stand for? __SEAS__

Underline the odd word out in each of these sets.
(Look carefully at the spelling **or** meaning of each word.)

Example
spring   <u>flung</u>   fling   string

31. hiss   moss   <u>his</u>   cross   miss
32. excite   exit   <u>entry</u>   exterior   exhibit
33. bonnet   cap   hat   <u>gloves</u>   bowler
34. mouth   ears   <u>skin</u>   nose   lips
35. calm   <u>chaotic</u>   peaceful   quiet   <u>still</u>

Which of the words in each set **cannot** be made using the letters of the word in capitals? Underline the word.

Example
PLATE   tea   tape   leap   <u>pail</u>

36. ELEPHANT   leant   hate   <u>happen</u>   path
37. FINANCE   face   <u>fancy</u>   inane   cane
38. GRUNTED   greet   dung   under   tuned
39. HAUNTS   shun   aunts   <u>shuts</u>   huts
40. IMMERSE   simmer   <u>miners</u>   mire   mere

PAPER 21

Underline the two words in each set that rhyme with the word in capitals.

Example

CAT　　mate　　<u>mat</u>　　freight　　pant　　<u>sat</u>

1. WENCH　　march　　<u>drench</u>　　wretch　　paunch　　<u>bench</u>
2. FLAME　　<u>game</u>　　lime　　lamb　　<u>same</u>　　famed
3. WALK　　croak　　bulk　　<u>talk</u>　　milk　　<u>chalk</u>
4. BUBBLE　　couple　　rouble　　<u>rubble</u>　　<u>trouble</u>　　stable
5. HAMPER　　<u>scamper</u>　　whimper　　<u>pamper</u>　　pauper　　paper

5/5

Which word in each set is most similar in meaning to the word in capitals? Underline the word.

Example

FAST　　hurry　　slow　　<u>quick</u>　　race

6. PICK　　cut　　take　　plant　　<u>pluck</u>
7. STOP　　<u>cease</u>　　ending　　noise　　wait
8. CHANT　　shout　　<u>sing</u>　　music　　hum
9. CARRIAGE　　horses　　driver　　lights　　<u>coach</u>
10. ABSENT　　permission　　present　　<u>away</u>　　here

5/5

Write these words into each grid so that they can be read across and down the grid.

Example

TOP　　TIN　　NAY　　PAY

T	O	P
I		A
N	A	Y

11. PAT   TEN   POT   TAN

P	A	T
O		A
T	E	N

12. LIE   ALL   AGE   EYE

A	L	L
G		I
E	Y	E

13. TUB   DOT   BIB   DAB

D	O	T
A		U
B	I	B

14. RUG   TOR   TOW   WIG

T	O	W
O		I
R	U	G

15. BOY   YEN   WIN   BOW

B	O	Y
O		E
W	I	N

5/5

Underline the word in the brackets that completes the second pair of words in the same way as the first pair.

Example

A is to B as one is to (to, <u>two</u>, too, three).

16. Five is to pentagon as six is to (square, dozen, pyramid, <u>hexagon</u>).

17. Oval is to circle as rectangle is to (kite, shape, trapezium, <u>square</u>).

18. Stone is to peach as pip is to (core, seed, peel, <u>apple</u>).

83

Paper 21

19. Rain is to drop as snow is to (blizzard, storm, drift, <u>flake</u>).

20. Blind is to seeing as deaf is to (ears, sound, <u>hearing</u>, music).

5 /5

Look carefully at these letter sequences. Work out the patterns to find the next letters in each sequence. The alphabet is here to help you.

A B C D E F G H I J K L M N O P Q R S T U V W X Y Z

Example

AB   DE   GH   JK   ?   <u>MN</u>

21. FG   JK   NO   RS   <u>VW</u>
22. RQ   RS   RP   RT   <u>RO</u>
23. BL   AK   ZJ   YI   <u>XH</u>
24. GKL FMN EOP DQR <u>CST</u>
25. AF   GB   CH   ID   <u>EJ</u>

5 /5

Look carefully at the given codes and work out the answers to the questions.

Example

If the code for SEAM is 3415, what does the code 341 stand for?   <u>SEA</u>

If the code for BELAY is 14235:

26. What is the code for BALE? <u>1324</u>

27. What does the code 154 stand for? <u>BYE</u>

28. What is the code for BELLY? <u>14225</u>

If the code for TREAT is 42314:

29. What is the code for RATE? <u>2143</u>

30. What does the code 4124 stand for? <u>TART</u>

5 /5

84

Paper 21

Underline the odd word out in each of these sets.
(Look carefully at the spelling **or** meaning of each word.)

Example
spring   <u>flung</u>   fling   string

31. sole   toe   <u>heal</u>   heel   ankle
32. squash   ale   tea   bread   water
33. bolt   <u>door</u>   lock   fasten   secure
34. palace   menace   <u>palate</u>   grimace   solace
35. helpful   cheerful   plentiful   tearful   <u>fulfil</u>

5/5

Which of the words in each set **cannot** be made using the letters of the word in capitals? Underline the word.

Example
PLATE   tea   tape   leap   <u>pail</u>

36. WHITHER   hire   <u>wheat</u>   white   their
37. ALPHABET   bath   <u>habit</u>   peal   path
38. BARRAGE   brag   gear   <u>brace</u>   grab
39. CONICAL   laconic   <u>local</u>   clan   lion
40. DIAMOND   main   <u>mean</u>   domain   amid

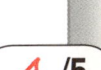

4/5

39/40

PAPER 22

Underline the two words in each set that rhyme with the word in capitals.

Example

CAT mate <u>mat</u> freight pant <u>sat</u>

1. STEEL <u>wheel</u> whole whelk realm <u>real</u>
2. BLOCK bloke <u>frock</u> croak <u>wok</u> crook
3. KNIT <u>nit</u> night pith <u>flit</u> nip
4. FOLDER mould elder <u>colder</u> <u>shoulder</u> fodder
5. BRAVE <u>gave</u> giver graze lay <u>waive</u>

Which word in each set is opposite in meaning to the word in capitals? Underline the word.

Example

HOT steaming warm frozen <u>cold</u>

6. SHARP point cut <u>blunt</u> blade
7. SHORT flowing wide small <u>long</u>
8. NORTH direction <u>south</u> east west
9. LOSE hunt <u>find</u> look mislay
10. WISE clever intelligent <u>foolish</u> ability

Which word in each set is most similar in meaning to the word in capitals? Underline the word.

Example

FAST hurry slow <u>quick</u> race

11. CUSHION pins velvet <u>pillow</u> sleep
12. BOUQUET ribbon <u>bunch</u> flowers special
13. MELODY <u>tune</u> harmony scale key
14. BEER drink bar <u>ale</u> bottle
15. PRICE expensive sale bargain <u>cost</u>

Write these words into each grid so that they can be read across and down the grid.

Example

TOP   TIN   NAY   PAY

T	O	P
I		A
N	A	Y

16. NOT   DEN   MAT   DAM

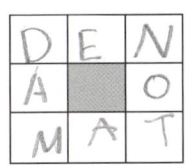

D	E	N
A		O
M	A	T

17. DIN   KID   PAN   KIP

K	I	D
I		I
P	A	N

18. KID   WAS   WOK   SAD

W	A	S
O		A
K	I	D

19. NOT   FEN   RAT   FOR

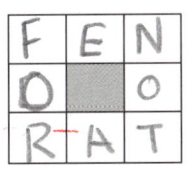

F	E	N
O		O
R	A	T

20. WIT   PIN   NET   PAW

P	A	W
I		I
N	E	T

5/5

Paper 22

In each sentence below, rearrange the word in capitals to make a properly spelt word that completes the sentences. Write the word on the answer line.

Example

The children were late for SLOHOC.   SCHOOL

21. The OPHIRCTEEL rescued the stranded climbers. HELICOPTER
22. She stuck the stamp onto the VEOPLENE and posted the card. ENVELOPE
23. They searched the KOPOROCLS to find baby hermit crabs. ROCKPOOLS
24. The sheep were grazing NEATBEH the apple trees. BENEATH
25. The WOKRIREFS lit up the sky. FIREWORKS

4/5

Look carefully at the given codes and work out the answers to the questions.

Example

If the code for SEAM is 3415, what does the code 341 stand for?   SEA

If the code for MONEY is 73658:

26. What is the code for NEON? 6536
27. What does the code 756 stand for? MEN

If the code for FARMER is 532412:

28. What is the code for FREE? 5211
29. What is the code for RARE? 2321
30. What does the code 52341 stand for? FRAME

5/5

Paper 22

Underline the odd word out in each of these sets.
(Look carefully at the spelling **or** meaning of each word.)

Example

spring   <u>flung</u>   fling   string

31. dog   hamster   <u>mosquito</u>   rabbit   pony
32. thyme   mint   <u>garden</u>   sage   parsley
33. midget   tiny   <u>statue</u>   small   petite
34. sorrow   borrow   morrow   <u>pillow</u>   barrow
35. kennel   <u>panel</u>   funnel   tunnel   fennel

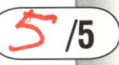

5/5

Which word in each set **cannot** be made using the letters of the word in capitals? Underline the word.

Example

PLATE   tea   tape   leap   <u>pail</u>

36. PLEASURE   please   leaps   lapse   <u>purple</u>
37. RALLIED   ride   <u>drear</u>   derail   dial
38. STUDENT   tents   <u>sudden</u>   dune   stun
39. TRANSFER   safer   faster   fears   <u>strain</u>
40. UNCOVER   <u>corner</u>   corn   rove   cone

5/5

39/40

33

Progress grid

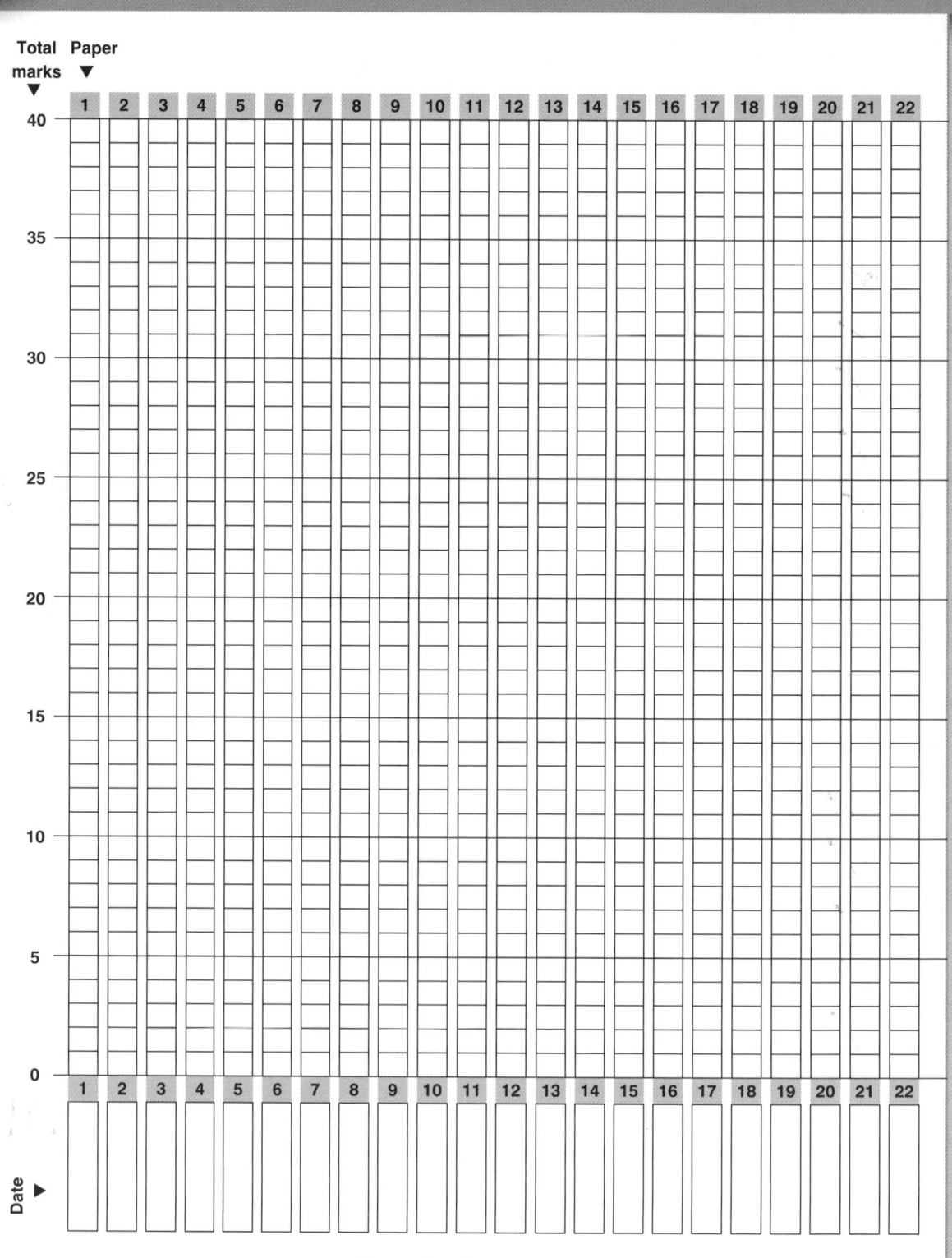

Now colour in your score!

Notes

Notes